D0112436

GRACE

R. T. KENDALL

GRACE

R. T. KENDALL

Charisma
HOUSE
A STRANG COMPANY

Most STRANG COMMUNICATIONS/CHARISMA HOUSE/SILOAM products are available at special quantity discounts for bulk purchase for sales promotions, premiums, fund-raising, and educational needs. For details, write Strang Communications/Charisma House/Siloam, 600 Rinehart Road, Lake Mary, Florida 32746, or telephone (407) 333-0600.

GRACE by R. T. Kendall
Published by Charisma House
A Strang Company
600 Rinehart Road
Lake Mary, Florida 32746
www.charismahouse.com

This book or parts thereof may not be reproduced in any form, stored in a retrieval system, or transmitted in any form by any means—electronic, mechanical, photocopy, recording, or otherwise—without prior written permission of the publisher, except as provided by United States of America copyright law.

Unless otherwise noted, all Scripture quotations are from the Holy Bible, New International Version. Copyright © 1973, 1978, 1984, International Bible Society. Used by permission.

Scripture quotations marked KJV are from the King James Version of the Bible.

Cover design by Karen Grindley

Copyright © 2006 by R. T. Kendall
All rights reserved

Library of Congress Cataloging-in-Publication Data:

Kendall, R. T.
  Grace / R.T. Kendall.
    p. cm.
  ISBN 1-59185-873-9 (pbk.)
  1. Grace (Theology) I. Title.

BT764.3.K46 2005
234--dc22
                                        2005026491

Previously published in Great Britain as *Just Grace* by the Society for Promoting Christian Knowledge, Holy Trinity Church, Marylebone Road, London NW1 4DU, ISBN 0-281-05224-7, copyright © 2000.

06 07 08 09 10 — 9 8 7 6 5 4 3 2 1
Printed in the United States of America

To Ernie and Margaret

CONTENTS

Preface

BOUT SIX YEARS ago I was having a conversation with myself that went like something like this: "I think I will stay at Westminster Chapel for exactly twenty-five years. Then I will retire. Louise and I will live in Key Largo, Florida. Since nobody knows me in America I will become a recluse and spend my time bonefishing twenty-four hours a day." I was not praying; I was only imagining.

At that moment the Holy Spirit spoke to me: "Your ministry in America will be to charismatics."

"Oh, no," I responded. For I wanted to reach evangelicals. I have the knowledge and also the credentials to reach evangelicals. They need what I have to offer, especially regarding the Holy Spirit.

But no, it would be a ministry largely to charismatics. Then the Lord seemed to point out to me, "Who was most qualified to reach Jews two thousand years ago? Was it not Paul the Apostle? Did he not have the knowledge to reach Jews, and did he not have the credentials?" But the Lord said to Paul, "Your ministry will be to Gentiles." He must have thought. *Oh, no, I want to reach my own people.* But Paul's ministry was largely to Gentiles. And though I do continue to get gracious invitations from evangelicals and non-charismatic churches, it is largely charismatics who beckon for my ministry. As to my time spent fishing, I did more of that when I came over to Florida in the summers when I was still at Westminster Chapel!

I can't be sure why God said that word to me. He doesn't speak to me like that every day. But one of the strongest confirmations of this word has not only been so many of my preaching invitations coming from churches regarded as charismatic, but also the amazing fact that Stephen Strang, publisher of Charisma House, has asked to publish virtually all of my books! The present book—*Grace*—is an example of this.

The funny thing is, I wrote *Grace* not with charismatics in mind. Not at all. It was written while I was still the minister of Westminster Chapel, and I had evangelicals in mind! Believe it or not, many of them do not have a solid understanding of either grace or the Law. Some of them would deny this, but I know what I am talking about. I wrote this book for them. It is an exposition of the Law of God with particular reference to the Ten Commandments and the New Testament doctrine of assurance. But I suspect all those who regard themselves as "charismatic" in some sense will profit from this book. This is because, sadly, so many Christians—whether evangelical or charismatic—are confused as to the meaning of the Law and its place in the *ordo salutis* (order of salvation).

My family and I went to England in 1973 not for me to be the minister of Westminster Chapel but to do the doctorate of philosophy in theology at Oxford University. I spent three years there immersed in the reformed doctrine of sanctification, faith, assurance, and the Law. I studied both the Reformers and the Puritans day and night for three years. It was they who gave us the historic Westminster Confession of Faith (1648). Though the book you now hold in your hands is not an academic book—it is written simply for all to understand—it is nonetheless part of the fruit of my doctoral studies at Oxford.

Called *Just Grace* when first published by SPCK in Great Britain, this book is now called, simply, *Grace*. I want to thank Alison Barr for the work she did when I was in London, and now I thank Debbie Marrie for her work over here. I must also thank Barbara Dycus for her hand in this publication and, of course, my friend Stephen Strang for publishing this book.

I warmly dedicate this book to Ernie and Margaret Paddon. They were most faithful prayer partners when I was the minister of Westminster Chapel. Ernie prayed for me an hour a day for the better part of my twenty-five years there. He was a deacon at the Chapel and church secretary for most of my time there. It was he who originally put the idea to me that I should preach on and write a book on the Ten Commandments. So here it is.

Preface

I hope this book will be a blessing to charismatic Christians as well as evangelicals. I pray for exactly this. As to why God would give me a ministry to charismatics in my own country, I am still not sure. You tell me!

—R. T. KENDALL
KEY LARGO, FLORIDA
www.rtkendallministries.com

Foreword

SHOULD WE APPLY grace or righteousness?" I was being asked a question at an open forum for leaders, and this one provided a real shock to my system. The questioner explained that an unmarried couple who was living together was asking about the possibility of being baptized at his church. The inquirer clearly saw grace and righteousness as alternatives—a serious mistake and one that the book in your hands ably addresses.

When God declared the first covenant obsolete (Heb. 8:13) and introduced a new covenant, He was not throwing in the towel in the battle against sin. He was revealing a new and better way of overcoming it. In the coming of Christ, grace suddenly "appeared" (from Greek *epiphany*, "shone out"), not to lower the standards but to equip believers to rise to unprecedented heights (Titus 2:11).

Not that God had not always been gracious. When Moses asked for a revelation of God, he was told that God's presence would pass before him and that God would reveal His name. So Moses heard, "The LORD, the LORD, the compassionate and gracious God, slow to anger" (Exod. 34:6). God has always been gracious. However, grace was particularly displayed in Christ's coming. The Law came by Moses, grace and truth came through Jesus Christ, and of His fullness we have all received grace upon grace. (See John 1:16–17.)

Grace certainly shone out in the coming of Christ, but grace does not come to lower the standard; it comes to motivate and enable us to live a totally new life. Paul told Titus that the grace of God appeared instructing us to say no to ungodliness (Titus 2:11–12).

Saying no is a vital part of holy living. The downward gravitational pull of human society is so all-pervasive that if we do not learn to say no we will soon be in trouble. If young women do not learn to say no they will be quickly compromised by the opposite sex. If young men do not learn to say no they will soon be experimenting with drugs and alcohol.

No is a word we must be instructed to say. It is an antisocial word. It goes against the tide. It takes courage and commitment to say it. It needs strong motivation, and grace motivates powerfully.

How does grace teach us? It begins by telling us that we are totally acceptable to God through our faith in Christ. We are justified freely as a gift. So I am a winner before I start. I am accepted before I have done anything. What a relief! How magnificent! Some would argue, "How dangerous!", but they do not understand. God starts by totally qualifying us. He will test us later, but He qualifies us first. We start accepted, qualified, and justified as a gift. The righteousness of Christ is freely given to me not only to start my Christian life but also every day of my life. He is the same yesterday, today, and forever. His totally righteous life of magnificent decisions—perfectly holy choices, steadfast purity in the face of fierce temptation—is totally credited to my account.

This is so encouraging that it is almost too good to be true. When I first heard the grace of God I felt like the early witnesses of the Resurrection. It says of them, "They could not believe for joy." I had lived in a school of tough and zealous commitment for quite a while. Condemnation was often overshadowing me. Trying harder was the way to succeed! School reports with their often repeated "could do better" and "should try harder" had a similar ring to my understanding of how to live the Christian life.

Suddenly I saw it! God's grace covers my failure and sin and justifies me freely as a gift. What a revelation! What joy! What thanksgiving and praise. Grace instructs me first by telling me I am a winner before I start.

Then grace tells you that Jesus wants you for His very own possession, His special treasure (Titus 2:14). God has a particular and personal delight in you. He chose you from before the foundation of the world. He foreknew you and predestined you to be His own. His Word says, "The LORD will take delight in you" (Isa. 62:4). God actually delights in you. He did not save you by mistake. He did not have to take you in a job lot. You were not born of human will but by the will of God. He will always love and cherish you.

Next, grace teaches us about the terrible price that was paid for our salvation. Those three simple words are so unfathomable in their depth: "He gave Himself." Some, motivated by kindness, might give a gift or even a fortune, but He gave Himself. He gave Himself to the human race. He gave Himself to a motley band of followers who would deny Him in His hour of need. He gave Himself to Satan's hour. He gave His cheek to those who tore out His beard, and He did not hide His face from spitting. He gave Himself to the full wrath of God, the total curse of the law. He gave Himself without reserve, though He was appalled in Gethsemane, though He shuddered at the shocking revelation of the bitterness of the cup. He sweated, as it were, great drops of blood, pleading with His Father that if it was possible it might be taken from Him. Yet He prevailed, determined to save us, and for the joy set before Him, He endured the cross, despising the shame. He became the center of mocking and shame from men and demons. He gave Himself to the sheer fury of a holy God who hates sin with a perfect loathing and fierce anger. The Son of God loved me and gave Himself for me.

Grace also teaches me what a glorious goal He has in mind. He wants a people red-hot for good deeds (Titus 2:14). He wants zealots. He hates lukewarmness. He would rather we were cold or hot. Lukewarmth makes Him vomit (Rev. 3:16). He wants passionate people burning with motivation and wholehearted in commitment. He gave His own life as our example. Zeal for His Father's house consumed Him.

God wants us red-hot for the works that He foreordained for us. He does not want mere busyness or hectic activity. He has prepared handpicked works for us. Grace teaches me that He chose the works in advance, and He wants me excitedly committed to doing them so that He can finally enthusiastically receive me to His eternal kingdom with the glorious words, "Well done, good and faithful servant."

Finally, grace teaches me that this world can be viewed simply as "this present age" (Titus 2:12). It is not permanent; it is just what is taking place now for a short while. We only live briefly. As a flower that buds, opens, fades, and quickly falls, so the very world itself is short-lived. This age is passing away. Grace opens my eyes to that reality. If I thought this life was going to last forever I might live differently, but I know it is brief. Eternity awaits. The new heavens and the new earth are ahead.

I often travel internationally and stay briefly in other countries. Often I do not fully unpack my case. I do not learn the language. Sometimes, if it is a particularly brief visit to Europe, I do not even change any money or even change my watch. Walking down the street I probably look like anyone else, but actually I do not belong! I do not fully identify. In a few days or hours I will not be there; I will be flying home again. I belong elsewhere!

Grace teaches me not to get my roots down too deeply in this temporary scene. Grace teaches me that it is easy to say no when I am not really part of the culture. I am a visiting alien; my citizenship is elsewhere. Not only do I not belong, but also I am eagerly anticipating another "appearing." Grace has "appeared" (Titus 2:11), but soon "the glorious appearing of our great God and Savior" will take place (v. 13). This full revelation will soon burst upon the world. He will come to be glorified in His saints and to be marveled at among all who have believed (2 Thess. 1:10).

Saying no to the world, the flesh, and the devil seems to make good sense when grace instructs me about all these things.

As Dr. Kendall clearly argues, the Law could never accomplish what grace so powerfully performs. With clear theological insight and warm pastoral application, RT demonstrates how Jesus came not to abolish the Law or the Prophets but to fulfill them through His own spotless life.

The authority of Christ's own words and the supply of the Holy Spirit inaugurate God's new arrangement for fellowship with His people. As RT points out, "If we walk in the Spirit, we will fulfill the Law 'accidentally,' even if we have never heard of the Ten Commandments!"

RT has given us a book of sound doctrine, personal warmth, and pastoral encouragement that genuinely serves those who long to live a life pleasing to God and enjoy the lavish grace that He supplies.

The Law commanded "thou shalt not." Grace came not to lower the standard but to change us from the inside, motivating, empowering, and teaching us to say no.

—TERRY VIRGO, FOUNDER
NEW FRONTIERS OF GREAT BRITAIN

Introduction

I CAME TO OXFORD from America with my family in 1973 to study my heroes—the Puritans. I thought I knew a little bit about them before I went, but I soon realized how little I knew. I was not prepared for what I discovered. Gradually my heroes began to fall, until the time I almost became disillusioned.

It is important for me to explain a bit of my background before you can appreciate this disappointment. I was brought up in a denomination, which I am still fond of and for which I thank God. I refer to the Church of the Nazarene, which was in some ways an offshoot of Methodism, founded by John Wesley. An Anglican clergyman, Wesley emphasized the immediate witness of the Holy Spirit in knowing you are truly saved and went on to teach his own brand of Christian perfectionism, or perfect love. Most Nazarenes admire John Wesley, as I did, and I never dreamed I would leave my old denomination. Some of their present leaders, knowing of my leaving them, feel I was not exposed to the true teaching of John Wesley, whose influence on them was important.

Be that as it may, I only know that I was taught that there were "two works of grace"—being "saved" and being "sanctified," to use Nazarene jargon. The former meant conversion and the forgiveness of my sins. Being saved, then, was the "first" work of grace. To be saved a person repented of all their sins—all you could literally think of, and then you trusted God to forgive you for the sake of Jesus' blood shed on the cross. This was also called justification or being justified by faith. This meant you were ready to go to heaven if you died—as long as you did not commit sin after that. For if you did, you were in a perilous state and could be eternally lost if you were not converted again.

My old denomination then taught that there was a "second" work of grace, which meant a cleansing from "inbred sin." The second work of grace was also to help ensure that one did not fall so easily. After all, if inbred sin was fully eradicated, as they taught, how could people sin? But they did! The other funny thing

1

was, the same instructions on how to be saved were also given to the same person who sought to be sanctified, namely, that one renounced all that was wrong in one's life and that he or she was as fully consecrated to God as one knew how. In other words, to be saved I had to say yes to God in all He required. The exact same thing was required to be sanctified. In those days I truly believed I had been saved and sanctified. The only problem was, I could still backslide after being sanctified and lose it all—which put me back to square one. The only way to keep sanctified was by not sinning, that is, by keeping the works of the Law. That is what I was brought up to believe.

Then, on October 31, 1955, something most extraordinary happened to me. I was nineteen and in my third year at Trevecca Nazarene College in Nashville, Tennessee. I was given the opportunity also to be the pastor of a small church in the mountains of East Tennessee—a little town called Palmer. I went there on weekends only. One Monday morning on my way back to Nashville I had what was almost like a "Damascus road" experience. The glory of the Lord filled my car. The person of Jesus was as real as if He were sitting next to me, and I entered into a rest of soul that exceeded anything I ever dreamed possible. What's more, my theology changed before the end of that day. I knew that I was eternally saved and that God had sovereignly operated on me by the Spirit. This led to my seeing that God had chosen me. In a word (though I did not know it at the time): I became a Calvinist, that is, I came to embrace predestination and election as well as the teaching of the eternal security of the believer. I also developed a consciousness of sin.

Up to that time, then, I believed not only in the two works of grace but also that you could lose your salvation if you sinned by breaking any of the Ten Commandments. I was told that forgiveness of sins came because Jesus died on the cross, but if I sinned I forfeited what He did for me. This meant that I had to keep myself saved by living a holy life—staying sanctified. I was always a very conscientious person, and I worried all the time whether I was still saved and sanctified, especially if I lost my temper (which I was always doing).

But my experience of October 31, 1955, changed all that. I just

2

knew I was saved. Forever. I was free. It was absolutely the most wonderful feeling in the world. "Is this a third work of grace, RT?" many asked. I did not know what to call it. I only knew I was saved. When I tried to point out my sense of security and the doctrine of election, I was warned, "You are going off into Calvinism." I did not know what that was (and did not care); I only knew something wonderful had happened to me. I also wondered if I was the first since the apostle Paul to believe and experience these things.

Within a year or so I was told that what had been revealed to me concerning the sovereignty of God was what the Puritans believed. This made me feel good. Very good. Every American knew about the Pilgrims who came over on the Mayflower, and the thought that I was now theologically akin to them was like a vindication. None of my friends or relatives were persuaded by any of my arguments, but I pointed out that people like the Puritans had been Calvinists. It set me to reading them, especially John Owen (1616–1685). I went to Oxford in 1973 to study John Owen's doctrine of the priestly work of Christ. It turned out that my thesis took a different direction, but it plunged me deep indeed into the Puritans.

I was not prepared for what I discovered. These men were so like the dear people of my old denomination I had left that I was stunned. Not that they taught all I used to believe, but it often came to the same thing. For no one could claim to be saved if they did not keep the works of the Law. Not that you could lose your salvation; it only meant you were not really converted in the first place if there was not a careful keeping of the Ten Commandments. After all, one dare not look directly to Christ for assurance—that would be presumptuous; one looked to his own faithfulness in keeping the Law first, and then—and only then—did one have the warrant to look to Christ for salvation. I kept telling myself that what these Puritans wrote surely was not what they appeared to be saying. I kept reading.

I remember it as though it were yesterday. I went to London to read since the Bodleian Library in Oxford did not have all the material I needed. I could take you to the very table at which I was sitting, except that the old British Library has now been removed to another place in London. I was reading Thomas Hooker

3

(1586-1647), who became the founder of the state of Connecticut. He championed the idea that the unbeliever must prepare himself for grace before he could become a Christian. "All roads lead to Rome," and all roads in this case led to the Ten Commandments. One of his contemporaries, Giles Firman (d. 1692), said it best: "Mr. Hooker, you make as good Christians before men are in Christ, as ever they are after would I were but as good a Christian now, as you make men while they are but preparing for Christ."[1] I continued to read Hooker until one afternoon, I took all I could take. I put my hands on the edge of that table in the British Library, pushed my chair back, stared at the ceiling—and asked myself, "Is this what I have come to this country for? Is this what I am to believe and preach?" I might as well have stayed like I was. I wanted to go out and shoot somebody! I turned in my books and went back to Oxford.

Most of the Puritans that I read can be described in this scenario: How do you know you are saved? By your sanctification. How do you know you have sanctification? By good works. How do you know what good works are? By the Ten Commandments.[2]

It is not that they believed you are saved by good works; it was merely that you could not know you are saved unless you kept the Ten Commandments. Martin Luther's discovery that we are justified by faith alone had sadly passed behind a cloud. The nature of assurance became the issue. You could not have assurance unless you kept the Law. If you were not keeping the Ten Commandments, you could not be a Christian.

I was also surprised to learn how so many of the Puritans died. William Perkins (1558-1602), the architectural mind for what became the tradition that led to the historic Westminster Confession of Faith, died "in the conflict of a troubled conscience." His immediate successor Paul Baynes (d. 1617) "went out of this world, with far less comfort than many weaker Christians enjoy." Sadly, this kind of dying testimony was not uncommon.[3]

That is certainly not what the Lord had shown me on my Monday morning journey back to Nashville. An immediate witness of the Holy Spirit assured me I was saved. My focus was on Christ. But the Puritans focused on themselves. As one actually put it, we know we are saved "by descending into ourselves to see whether we are sanctified." Sooner or later, everything centered on the Law. One influential man at the time, John Dod, was actually known as "John the Decalogue," which literally means "John the Ten Commandments."

I am sorry to say that, for a while, I had a love/hate relationship with the Ten Commandments. This was not helped when in 1984, after seven years at Westminster Chapel, I was formally accused of antinomianism by some former deacons. Antinomianism (literally "against law") is the idea that it does not matter how you live if you are saved. That is certainly not what I preached, and I knew I was no antinomian (a very serious charge). But this is what was put to me partly because I do believe we are saved by faith alone and our assurance of being a Christian is not traced to the Ten Commandments but to Christ alone.

I have had to think through very carefully what I believe. Our critics can be good for us; they keep us on our toes! I have sought to know as much as possible exactly what Jesus taught in the Sermon on the Mount and what the apostle Paul taught, especially in Galatians and Romans.

It is not an easy thing to get the correct balance between the Law and the gospel.

> Whoever knows how to distinguish skillfully between the Law and the Gospel, by the grace of God he also knows how to be a theologian.
> —MARTIN LUTHER

> Anybody who wishes to be a theologian must distinguish between Law and Gospel.
> —MARTIN LUTHER

> There is no man living on earth who knows how to distinguish between the Law and the Gospel.
> —MARTIN LUTHER

I pray this book will show we are getting our balance nearly right and that God will bless you as you read it.

Chapter 1

A STUNNING CLAIM

> Do not think that I have come to abolish the Law
> or the Prophets; I have not come to abolish them
> but to fulfill them.
>
> —MATTHEW 5:17

NO ONE WAS prepared for Jesus' view of the Law. Nobody living in Israel at the time had ever heard anything like it. The above verse is Jesus' first mention of the Law in the New Testament. It comes near the beginning of the most famous sermon ever preached, which St. Augustine called the "Sermon on the Mount."

JESUS' PRESENTATION OF THE LAW

What Jesus had to say about the Law did not please anybody. As we will see, His view did not please those who wanted to do away with the Law, nor did it please those who "loved" it. He elbowed in on the Pharisees' territory. They fancied themselves to be the experts in this matter, and yet what He had to say they hadn't even thought of.

A great anointing of the Spirit always does this, particularly in preaching. What makes preaching truly outstanding is that it forces me to see truth I hadn't seen before or even conceived. Rather than a speaker churning out the same old clichés that defend a party line, what is dazzling to any hearer is an unveiling of a text you thought you knew backward and forward but which is made new and freshly relevant. The reason the apostle Paul could speak of the "unsearchable riches of Christ" (Eph. 3:8) is because God's Word is inexhaustible. The Holy Spirit alone can do this with any text, and since Jesus had the Spirit without any limit (John 3:34), He could say better than any what no one had seen or heard (1 Cor. 2:9).

Jesus stunned the Sadducees in the same manner. Although the Sadducees are not mentioned in the Sermon on the Mount, Jesus had a way of bringing understanding to a text that never crossed their minds either. You could not have told the Sadducees that they had anything new to learn about Exodus 3:6—"I am the God of your father, the God of Abraham, the God of Isaac and the God of Jacob"—but Jesus showed them what they had never considered, namely, that it meant Abraham, Isaac, and Jacob were alive and well! "He is not the God of the dead but of the living." All were "astonished" at His teaching. (See Matthew 22:23–33.) But the Pharisees and teachers of the Law (also known as the scribes) outnumbered the Sadducees, and this may be the reason He refers to them as He does in the Sermon on the Mount.

It is interesting how Jesus brought up the subject of the Law. Until now, He had apparently not referred to it, either explicitly or implicitly. Then almost out of the blue He says, "Do not think that I have come to abolish the Law or the Prophets." Were they really thinking that He might? What made Jesus say this? Why say it here?

The question follows, then, is the Law really a new subject in this sermon? Jesus began the sermon with the beatitudes (Matt. 5:3–10), then followed the reference to our being salt and light. That led to the exhortation, "Let your light shine before men, that they may see your good deeds and praise your Father in heaven" (Matt. 5:16). "Good deeds" could have suggested the Law. So, was Jesus suddenly changing the subject by bringing up the Law, or was it the culmination of what He was building up to? Does He say, "Do not think that I have come to abolish the Law and the

Prophets" because they were thinking it? Or was it because they should have thought it in the light of what He had been saying?

As for the beatitudes, there was no apparent need to keep the Law in order to be poor in spirit, to mourn, to be meek, or to hunger and thirst after righteousness. The Law was not an obvious ingredient in any of these graces. They were surely possible without the Law, indeed, as though the Law had never come in the first place.

Abraham had exhibited the graces of the beatitudes over four hundred years before the Law came. Long before Abraham, Enoch had walked with God (Gen. 5:22) and pleased God (Heb. 11:5). Noah walked with God (Gen. 6:9) and demonstrated obedience of faith before the Law came (Heb. 11:7). As for Abraham, he not only believed God (Gen. 15:6) and obeyed Him (Heb. 11:8), but he also showed extraordinary faith and patience in waiting for the fulfillment of the promise and experienced an utter intimacy with God (Heb. 6:13–14). All this was before the Law was given to Israel (Gal. 3:16–19).

If you look at each of the beatitudes in their progressive order, you will see that what Jesus taught could have been experienced had the Law never been given to Moses or Israel at all. It is therefore possible that some astute and theologically acute listeners would be thinking, *No Law is needed for this kind of teaching.* Jesus may have discerned that they were thinking, *If we get on board with the teaching we have heard so far, we certainly do not need the Law of Moses.* The beatitudes, the need to be salt and light and showing good works (Matt. 5:13–16), could have been carried out had there been no Moses. The people might, therefore, have begun to conclude: He is going to do away with the Law.

If they had not already wondered this, then perhaps Jesus is implying that they should have thought it. We only know that He abruptly says, "Do not think I have come to abolish the Law and the Prophets."

THE LAW IS TO BE FULFILLED

There is yet another possible reason Jesus said this: rumors were going around that the long-awaited Messiah would suddenly appear and immediately abolish the Mosaic Law. Jesus was being seen as the apocalyptic figure, one who came on the scene suddenly—showing discontinuity with the past and bringing direct revelation from God. Rumors of such an apocalyptic figure— sometimes thought to be the Son of man (from the prophet Daniel)—were common. This person, some apparently hoped, would inaugurate a new era and then abolish the Law. The Messiah would start all over again, as it were, with something else. These beatitudes looked ominously like such a new way of thinking. No one had ever heard teaching like it.

It follows, therefore, that some people were possibly thinking: this man could be the Messiah, and His teaching is looking very much like one that could be carried out without the Law.

Jesus' words, "Do not think that I have come to abolish the Law or the Prophets; I have not come to abolish them but to fulfill them" (Matt. 5:17), must also have poured cold water on the fervent hopes of revolutionaries who were about. These included people who loved any new forms of teaching and who jumped at any opportunity to overturn everything. The idea of overthrowing the Law would appeal to many people like this. Some people, not necessarily dedicated to truth, merely get tired of the status quo and tradition and welcome almost anything that appears radical. Could people like this not be whom Jesus described later on when He observed that the kingdom of heaven suffers "violence" (Matt. 11:12, KJV). There has been a trend both to translate and interpret this to cohere with the idea that laying hold of the kingdom is what Jesus commended.[1] (See also Luke 16:16.) Surely Jesus was merely making an observation that has sadly been repeated many times in church history: people with misguided zeal often run ahead of their leaders and set back, rather than advance, the cause of the glory of God.

For example, I saw this sort of thing happen many times in Westminster Chapel. The church was very traditional. While pastoring this church, I often said that England was the most traditional country in the world and that Westminster Chapel was the most traditional church in England! We had been in "no-man's-land" for a number of years, especially since I invited Arthur Blessitt, the man who has carried a twelve-foot cross around the world, to preach for us. He turned us upside-down, but we never became a charismatic church. We were wide open to the Holy Spirit while making expository preaching central to all we stood for. We moved slowly, but definitely, over the years from the traditional style of worship we had become accustomed to. Some think we moved too quickly; some think we moved too slowly. I carefully taught our people in order to hold back as many as possible while also making important changes. We had a degree of success; after all, I was there for twenty-five years! But my point is this: those who think we moved too slowly were as difficult to handle as those who felt we should have made no changes at all. Because we were open to the Holy Spirit some thought we should have been charismatics like so many churches. They showed little patience with those who were traditionally minded, and sometimes were even less patient with me because I tried to keep the boat from rocking more violently than necessary. Moreover, if I invited, say, Arthur Blessitt to preach, you could expect a hundred or more people to turn up out of the blue—for one service only, and they would virtually take over. They would arrive early, get the best seats, have their hands in the air in worship—and put off the rest of us. They seemed to want to make a statement: "We'll show these people at Westminster Chapel how things should be done and how to have revival!" Never mind that our own people fasted and prayed behind the scenes, came out on the streets on Saturdays to witness, and dedicated themselves to a close walk with God. The Chapel "suffered violence" by those people who, if anything, set our progress back. They were sincere but misguided. They also loved the idea of Westminster Chapel being less formal and felt called to hasten our move in their direction. This sort of thing happened to us countless times—it hurts more than helps, and church history is ridden with accounts where people felt that a new movement of God was not going far enough or fast enough.

In any case, there are always those of a revolutionary, radical mind-set who love the idea of uprooting time-honored foundations and values, including the Law. It is likely that Jesus had people like this in mind as well when He sent a signal early on in His ministry that He had not come to do away with the Law at all. This must have punctured their balloon.

How does this make you feel? Are you disappointed that Jesus did not abolish the Law then and there? Would you have been pleased had He rendered the Law null and void, then started all over again, perhaps with a new and different ethic? Are you unhappy with the Ten Commandments? Would you add one or two—or take some of them out altogether?

THE AUTHORITY OF JESUS

Jesus made a statement that showed there would be a necessary connection between Himself and all that Moses gave to Israel. He therefore affirmed Moses and the whole of the Law. Then He added, "or the Prophets." Why did He bring in the Prophets? Were they a bone of contention, too? Yes. They had long been regarded as rivals to the priesthood. The priesthood dates back to the giving of the Law at Sinai as well. The Sadducees regarded themselves as the successors to Zadok the ancient priest who anointed Solomon as king (1 Kings 1:39). The Sadducees generally disliked the Prophets but would not have wanted the Law abolished.

Had Jesus affirmed the Law but not the Prophets, the Sadducees would have been interested. There was a rivalry between the Sadducees and the Pharisees. The Sadducees had more prestige; the Pharisees were greater in number. The Pharisees affirmed the Prophets. Therefore, the Sadducees would have been delighted had Jesus shown contempt for the Prophets. But no; He had not come to nullify the Prophets either. As a result Jesus' statement in Matthew 5:17 pleased nobody.

This is also the first time in the Sermon on the Mount that Jesus refers to Himself. One may ask, who does He think he is— imagining that people would think that He might even have the power to abolish the Law or the Prophets had He wanted to? But He knew all eyes were fastened on Him. He knew who He was in any case—and why He had arrived on the scene. And yet, though neither a member of the Sanhedrin nor a Sadducee, He implied unashamedly that He certainly did have the right to do whatever He planned even though the Law had been in existence for thirteen hundred years. His authority was a self-conscious authority but without the slightest trace of arrogance or presumption.

Anybody else talking like this would have been arrogant. But Jesus was the opposite of arrogance. He was unpretentious. That, to me, is a part of His glory. A proof of this is seen in the first person to approach Him as soon as the sermon was over. Large crowds followed Him. But it was a leper who came and knelt before Him. A leper in those days knew his place. People dreaded leprosy and ran in the other direction when they saw a leper. But that leper knew he could get away with going straight to Jesus. Why? He saw unpretentiousness in Jesus and knew he would be accepted. He was right. When he said, "Lord, if you are willing, you can make me clean," Jesus responded, "I am willing," and healed the man (Matt. 8:1–3). Had Jesus spoken arrogantly by His claim in Matthew 5:17, that leper would have never wanted to approach Jesus. Moses was said to be the humblest man of any at the time (Num. 12:3), and so too the "new" Moses.

The words, "Do not think that I have come" show a self-conscious arrival. He knows He has come "for such a time as this" for a strategic purpose. He might have said He had been sent; such language is used in the Gospel of John. (See John 3:17.) He only says "I have come," but in saying this He effectively announces a new era. It marked the end of a 1,300-year *parenthesis*—a word and concept I will now explain.

Paul stated that the Law was "added" (Rom. 5:20; Gal. 3:19), referring to its emergence some 430 years after the time of Abraham. The promise to Abraham was actually the "gospel" (Gal. 3:8). Abraham saw the day of Christ and was "glad," said Jesus (John 8:56). The introduction of the Law 430 years after Abraham's time had not at all done away with the promise to Abraham. The Law therefore was parenthetical—added—"until the Seed [namely, Christ] to whom the promise referred had come" (Gal. 3:19). It was added because of the "transgressions" of Israel (Gal. 3:19). Therefore the gospel of Christ is the same promise that had been made to Abraham—as though there had been no Law at all.

Abraham knew that what had been promised to him would be fulfilled by a person traceable to himself. The promise to him, as he tried to count the stars, referred to his "offspring" (Gen. 15:5), that is, seed, meaning one person. Paul stresses this: "The promises were spoken to Abraham and to his seed. The Scripture

13

does not say 'and to seeds,' meaning many people, but 'and to your seed,' meaning one person, who is Christ" (Gal. 3:16). That is why Jesus said Abraham saw the day of Christ and was glad. By revelation of the Holy Spirit, then, Abraham was given to see that the countless stars, although it meant a posterity that could not be counted, would be a people saved by one person who was "still in his body," to use the language of Hebrews 7:10. As it happened, that one person, Jesus Christ, came approximately 1,700 years later when He was born of the Virgin Mary.

THE LAW IS TO BE SURPASSED

But the big point Paul wants to make is that not only is there an unbroken continuity between Abraham and Christ, but also the Law—which came in between the two events—did not change anything at all. "What I mean is this: The law, introduced 430 years later, does not set aside the covenant previously established by God and thus do away with the promise" (Gal. 3:17). For when God made His promise to Abraham it was with Jesus Christ in mind—then and there. As it turned out, it was necessary for God to bring in the Law. But the promise to Abraham was not nullified, or "set aside," as Paul put it. It was still intact—as though there had been no Law at all!

The Law, then, was but a parenthesis in salvation history. A parenthetical phrase (text within parentheses, such as this) can be left out of a sentence without changing the meaning, although what is in the parentheses can make the meaning clearer. So that 1,300-year parenthesis—the existence of the Law—was a part of God's plan. The problem was, that Law had never been "fulfilled." That means that it always looked beyond itself. It awaited fulfillment. It needed someone to do what had never been done, namely, keeping it perfectly and fulfilling its intentions. In other words, even though the Law was "added," which made it a parenthesis, it became "a yoke" upon the necks of the people of Israel from the first day. Peter therefore said that neither Jews living in the first century nor the ancient Israelites were able to bear it (Acts 15:10). It haunted them day and night. Whether it be the moral, civil, or ceremonial Law, it was unfulfilled and could not go away until its demands be totally satisfied. It demanded to be reckoned with. Like it or not, even though it was a parenthesis, it would not go away until somebody came along and did what no human being had ever done.

JESUS IS THE FULFILLMENT OF THE LAW

It was at this point in the Sermon on the Mount, then, that Jesus made what Dr. Martyn Lloyd-Jones reckons was the most stupendous claim Jesus ever made: "Do not think that I have come to abolish the Law or the Prophets; I have not come to abolish them but to fulfill them" (Matt. 5:17). In one stroke of utterance Jesus not only put to silence any rumor that He would do away with the Law, but He also showed that there was no discord between His teaching and the Law. Indeed, there was a direct connection between Himself and the Law. Because He would, by fulfilling it, mark the end of that 1,300-year parenthesis.

As we will see further below, Jesus still had to make good this promise. It was an extraordinary claim to make, but there would be a further waiting period before He would close that parenthesis—by His death.

The Greek word *katalusi* that translates "abolish" means "to abrogate or nullify." Had Jesus said He would abolish the Law it would have rendered the Law and the Prophets useless, out-of-date, or irrelevant. But by saying He would not abolish the Law—or the Prophets—but fulfill them, He showed that they were incomplete without His arriving on the scene. He therefore showed that they had always represented unfinished business; they pointed beyond themselves and required what He Himself would fulfill. They needed to be succeeded, and Jesus now claims He is the one to do that.

> In one stroke of utterance Jesus not only put to silence any rumor that He would do away with the Law, but He also showed that there was no discord between His teaching and the Law.

The word *fulfill* (Greek, *plerosai*) means to bring about the event to which the Law and the Prophets pointed. "The Law and the Prophets" in a sense was Jesus' way of summarizing the whole of the Old Testament. This further shows the stunning nature of His statement in Matthew 5:17. "I am the fulfillment of the Old Testament" is what He was really saying. And yet He was saying even more than that. For the Law had not been fulfilled—for two reasons. First, no one had ever really kept it. Second, the very content of the Law showed it was incomplete. As for the Prophets, they pointed to one who was to come. "I am that person," Jesus was saying.

But Matthew 5:17 was also a prophecy. Jesus was stating prophetically what He would do. He hadn't done it yet, that is, at the time He stated this. He had perhaps two or three years left. It is not certain how old He was when He preached this sermon, that is, how long He had been on the public scene. Perhaps He was barely over thirty. If He was thirty-three when He died, we can project that He had some two years or so in which to keep His promise to fulfill the Law.

When Jesus used the words, "I have come," He was referring to the purpose of His coming from heaven to earth. He anticipated a certain mission. *Mission* means the work for which one has been "sent."

Consider therefore the work cut out for Jesus when He made this extraordinary statement. He promised to fulfill the statutes of the Law; all its rules. The Law is generally considered to include three things: moral (the Ten Commandments), civil (the way Israel was to govern itself), and ceremonial (regulations pertaining to the worship of God). He promised personally to attain to the standard of the Law—a very high standard indeed, which, as I said, nobody had achieved. This also meant the specifications of the Law that included over two thousand verses of legislation from Exodus, Leviticus, Numbers, and Deuteronomy. There would be complete and total obedience—by Himself—to these specifications without the slightest deviation. There would be a careful scrutiny of His life and work, for it followed that He must fulfill the minutest requirements. The Law pronounced death on anyone who did not keep it to the full: "Cursed is the man who does not uphold the words of this law by carrying them out" (Deut. 27:26).

The writer of Hebrews says, "The law is only a shadow of the good things that are coming—not the realities themselves. For this reason it can never, by the same sacrifices repeated endlessly year after year, make perfect those who draw near to worship" (Heb. 10:1). The Law pointed to a fulfillment that no priest or worshiper had ever managed to accomplish. If it had achieved fulfillment, "would they not have stopped being offered?" Had the sacrificial system really worked, "the worshipers would have been cleansed once for all, and would no longer have felt guilty for their sins" (v. 2). The truth is, the sacrifices of the Law were repeated year after year without perfecting those who worshiped.

This shows more clearly why the statement of Jesus in Matthew 5:17 was so unusual. Not only would He perfectly keep the Ten Commandments, but also He become the fulfillment of the ancient sacrificial system. He would in the meantime have to fulfill all the Mosaic legislation. For example, He would keep the festivals of Israel three times a year. He kept the Jewish Sabbath every Saturday of His life. He would keep the "new moons," the "seventh year," Passover and the feast of unleavened bread, the feast of Pentecost, tabernacles, trumpets, and Day of Atonement. He would also have to be that prophet of whom Moses spoke, "The LORD your God will raise up for you a prophet like me from among your own brothers. You must listen to him" (Deut. 18:15). He would therefore be the "new" Moses.

As for "fulfilling the Prophets," this had begun by being born of a virgin (Isa. 7:14; Luke 1:34). His parents ensured that the Law was kept while Jesus was a baby and growing up (Luke 2:21–24, 41). He would be the suffering servant foreseen by Isaiah (Isa. 53), a task that lay ahead. In the meantime He must never sin at all—in thought, word, or deed. Far from abolishing the Law and Prophets, says Jesus, "I have come to fulfill them." Never before had anybody made such a claim. Never had people heard such a claim. What Jesus promised to do—fairly early on in His public ministry—had never been done.

Jesus kept His word. How? First, He standardized the Law; that is, He upheld the standard of morality that the Law demanded. Far from doing away with what some hoped would be abolished, Jesus made it abundantly clear: the level of righteousness and rule for living of the people of God would not be changing!

Jesus therefore submitted to the Law. Having been born under the Law He bowed to it willingly. Rather than make Himself above the Law He accepted it all—from the Ten Commandments to those two thousand verses of legislation that are found in Exodus, Leviticus, Numbers, and Deuteronomy. He actually submitted to the Law before He entered the Virgin Mary's womb: "A body you prepared for me" (Heb. 10:5). The Word—as Jesus was called before He was born—agreed to become flesh.

Jesus also fulfilled the Law by sinlessness. To make good His promise to fulfill the Law, He would never sin—not once. He would be the first and last person on Earth never to sin. Even Pontius Pilate was forced to say, "I find no basis for a charge against him," or as the King James Version puts it, "I find no fault in him" (John 19:4). So Peter quoted Isaiah and said, "He committed no sin, and no deceit was found in his mouth" (1 Pet. 2:22). As the writer of Hebrews says, "For we do not have a high priest who is unable to sympathize with our weaknesses, but we have one who has been tempted in every way, just as we are—yet was without sin" (Heb. 4:15). He is "holy, blameless, pure, set apart from sinners" (Heb. 7:26).

This therefore meant that Jesus personally kept every one of the Ten Commandments we will examine in this book. He was never remotely guilty of idolatry. As for the first commandment ("You shall have no other gods before me" [Exod. 20:3]), He worshiped and listened to the Father only. "Whatever the Father does the Son also does" (John 5:19). "By myself I can do nothing; I judge only as I hear, and my judgment is just, for I seek not to please myself but him who sent me" (v. 30). "I always do what pleases him" (John 8:29). As for the second commandment, He bowed only to the Father (Exod. 20:4–6). He never misused the Father's name (v. 7). He kept the Sabbath (vv. 8–11). He honored His parents (v. 12), even ensuring His mother's care moments before He died (John 19:27). He never killed anybody (Exod. 20:13)—He did not even hate. He never committed adultery (v. 14)—He did not even lust. He never stole, never lied, and never coveted (vv. 15–17). He was sinless. Instead of losing His temper when they scoffed at Him on the cross, He prayed: "Father, forgive them, for they do not know what they are doing" (Luke 23:34).

The penalty of the Law was the death sentence in fulfillment against capital sins. All our greatest sins—blasphemy, murder, and adultery—were charged to Jesus. It was the will of the Lord "to crush him and cause him to suffer" (Isa. 53:10). He was indeed "stricken" and "smitten" by God for what we have done (v. 4). That is why He died. The penalty of the Law was carried out against Him.

JESUS HAS TAKEN OUR PLACE UNDER THE LAW

Jesus fulfilled the Law, therefore, by being our substitute. All He did—in life and in death—was for us. He did it all for us. He took our place under the Law. His holy life became our sanctification (1 Cor. 1:30). His baptism was for us. When He was next in line to be baptized, John—who called for a baptism of repentance— could not understand why Jesus would ask to be baptized. It was for us—"to fulfill all righteousness" (Matt. 3:15). His keeping the Law was our keeping the Law. His perfection was our perfection. His righteousness was our righteousness. His obedience was our obedience (Rom. 5:15, 19). He even believed perfectly for us (John 4:34; Heb. 2:13), which is why the righteousness of God is revealed from faith (His faith) to faith (our faith) (Rom. 1:17; 3:22; Galatians 2:16–20).[2]

As our substitute, Jesus suffered. The physical pain of a Roman crucifixion was unspeakably torturous—almost certainly the most excruciating pain ever devised by wicked men. On top of the physical suffering came the worst moment of all: when His Father deserted Him. At some point in time on Good Friday— between noon and three o'clock—all our sins were transferred to Jesus as though He were guilty. In Martin Luther's words, He became legally the world's greatest sinner—by imputation, that is, our sins were charged to Him. "God made him who had no sin to be sin for us, so that in him we might become the righteousness of God" (2 Cor. 5:21). "About the ninth hour Jesus cried out in a loud voice, *'Eloi, Eloi, lama sabachthani?'*—which means, 'My God, my God, why have you forsaken me?'" (Matt. 27:46).

As it was true that never a man spoke as this man, it was also true: never a man suffered as this man.

> We may not know, we cannot tell
> What pains he had to bear;

We only know it was for us
He hung and suffered there.[3]

The seed of the woman (Gen. 3:15; Gal. 3:19) became our Passover lamb (1 Cor. 5:7). All of the sacrifices of the ancient Mosaic system were but "shadows" of things to come (Heb. 10:1). Jesus was the fulfillment of those animals—bulls, goats, lambs, pigeons. As we saw above, those sacrifices had to be repeated year after year. And as I said, that alone should have been a sufficient hint in ancient Israel that there must be more to come. On that Good Friday when, after living thirty-three years without sin— and after several hours of flogging and false accusations—God's Lamb took away the sin of the world (John 1:29), Jesus became the fulfillment of the Law and the Prophets.

Mission accomplished. Jesus said, "It is finished" (John 19:30). No sooner had He uttered these words than the veil of the temple was torn in two from top to bottom and bodies of some saints arose and walked around Jerusalem (Matt. 27:51–53).

Jesus did yet another thing by His substitutionary death: He satisfied the divine justice through the shedding of His blood. Charles Spurgeon used to say that there is no gospel apart from these two words—we should put them into our theological vocabularies—*substitution* and *satisfaction*. God's justice had never been satisfied until Jesus shed His own blood. The one thing that had not been satisfied since Adam and Eve fell in the Garden of Eden was God's justice. This, too, Jesus came to do—and did.

JESUS SURPASSES THE LAW

Jesus not only fulfilled the Law and the Prophets, but He also succeeded them. Indeed, He exceeded the Law; His life and example went beyond anything thought of by the standard and expectations of the Law. No one lived as Jesus lived; no one loved as Jesus loved. His life exceeded the Law; even beyond the best of the holy men of old. His example set a new standard of righteousness. It was the righteousness of the kingdom of heaven, the righteousness of the realm of the Spirit, which would surpass that of the teachers of the Law and Pharisees.

So, then, far from abolishing the Law, He outclassed the Law. What Paul could call "Christ's law" (1 Cor. 9:21) went beyond anything dreamed of by the Law and the Prophets. What is more, those people who dwell in the realm of the ungrieved Holy Spirit continue the standard set by Jesus. Not that one is sinless—far from it. For "if we claim to be without sin, we deceive ourselves and the truth is not in us" (1 John 1:8). And yet Jesus died and "condemned sin in sinful man, in order that the righteous requirements of the law might be fully met in us, who do not live according to the sinful nature but according to the Spirit" (Rom. 8:3–4).

Chapter 2

THE DESTINY OF THE LAW

I tell you the truth, until heaven and earth
disappear, not the smallest letter, not the least
stroke of a pen, will by any means disappear
from the Law until everything is accomplished.

—MATTHEW 5:18

AVING MADE THE truly astonishing prophecy that He
would actually fulfill the Law and the Prophets, in the
above verse Jesus demonstrates that He knows very well
the extraordinary work cut out for Him. Matthew 5:18 is but an
elaboration of the previous verse. The Greek word *gar*—which
means "for"—is strangely omitted in the New International
Version. In the Greek it shows the connection. It should read,
"For I tell you the truth," namely, that every detail of the Law just
mentioned in Matthew 5:17 would be fulfilled.

JESUS FULFILLS THE LAW

Not one idle comment was given to Moses when He wrote down
the Law, word for word, at Mount Sinai. Those two thousand verses
have a definite purpose. "Not the smallest letter" refers to the ninth
letter of the Greek alphabet, *iota*. The well-known phrase "one iota
of difference" refers to this Greek letter, which is the smallest in

the Greek alphabet.[1] It may also refer to the Hebrew *yod*, which is a base mark, the smallest letter in the Hebrew alphabet. "The least stroke of a pen" is the translation of *keraia*, which probably refers to the Hebrew word *waw*. It goes to show that Jesus has the highest possible view of divine inspiration of the Old Testament. Nothing will be overlooked or left undone. "The Scripture cannot be broken" (John 10:35). "Heaven and earth will pass away, but my words will never pass away" (Matt. 24:35).

Jesus introduces this verse with a solemn declaration: "I tell you the truth." The King James Version says, "Verily I say unto you." The Greek word *amen*—also a Hebrew word—and spoken by Jesus in Aramaic, means "certainly." God always tells the truth (Heb. 6:18), and Jesus claims to say or do nothing but what He sees the Father doing (John 5:19). But when He takes the time to say, "I tell you the truth," whereas it does not make the statement "more true," it does indicate a matter of great importance. It is virtually the equivalent of declaring an oath which has as its purpose putting "an end to all argument" (Heb. 6:16). Jesus uses *amen* differently from anyone else before Him. This is a word that is generally used at the end of a prayer. One also says amen if you agree with what was just said. (See Deuteronomy 27:15–26.) But Jesus uses it to introduce what He is about to say—to strengthen His own word: "I tell you the truth." It is the ancient way of saying, "Thus saith the Lord," having the force of Elijah or Moses.

THE LAW DISAPPEARS

It is now that Jesus is prepared to elaborate on this daring statement of Matthew 5:17 in which He promised to fulfill the ancient Mosaic Law—the Ten Commandments plus two thousand pieces of legislation—by Himself. He speaks of a scheduled disappearance. Twice in this verse He uses the word *disappear*: "I tell you the truth, until heaven and earth disappear, not the smallest letter, not the least stroke of a pen, will by any means disappear from the Law until everything is accomplished." Two things are scheduled to disappear: one is the present universe, and the other is the specifications of the Law that He had come to fulfill. Heaven and earth will disappear at the Second Coming. The specifications of the Law will disappear once Jesus has finished His work. This is why we are not under the Law as Jesus was.

You will note above that the word *until* is also used twice. The first use of *until* refers to the time in between—as long as the Law is unfulfilled. That means when the Law is fulfilled, something can then be ready to disappear, namely the universe. The second use of *until* refers to the disappearance of the need for anybody else to keep the specifications of the Law. For once everything is accomplished by Jesus' own perfect performance, the sacrifices and detailed minutiae of the Law would not have to be kept. This is why Peter, when addressing the Jerusalem council, pointed out that the Law was a "yoke that neither we nor our fathers have been able to bear" (Acts 15:10).

Therefore when Jesus refers to the "least stroke of a pen"—the *iota* or *yod*—He was not referring to the morality of the Law (the Ten Commandments) but minutiae of righteousness. For example, diet restrictions such as not cooking a young goat in its mother's milk (Exod. 23:19), or not eating pork (Lev. 11:7–8) or shellfish (Lev. 11:9–12). This means that, since Jesus fulfilled the Law, I eat pork, rabbit, shrimp, and lobster! Certain dress codes can be ignored: "Do not wear clothing woven of two kinds of material" (Lev. 19:19). I can wear a silk tie with a wool suit! I can also cut my sideburns and edges of my beard, if I wear a beard (Lev. 19:27). I do not have to obey strict agricultural laws if I am a farmer (Lev. 19:19) or keep the feasts in Jerusalem three times a year (Exod. 23:14–17). Best of all, I do not have to worry about various offerings: burnt offerings, grain offerings, fellowship offerings, sin offerings, or guilt offerings (Lev. 1:17; 2:1–16; 3:1–17; 4:1–5:13; 5:14–6:7). Once Jesus fulfilled these I am free from them. He kept them for me.

In a word, Jesus announced a scheduled disappearance; once He fulfilled the Law these things disappeared. And yet even before He Himself fulfilled the Law and all its minutiae, He gave hints along the way that things would change for all of us. For Jesus declared all foods "clean" (Mark 7:19). This is why Paul later said, "Therefore do not let anyone judge you by what you eat or drink, or with regard to a religious festival, a New Moon celebration or a Sabbath day. These are a shadow of the things that were to come; the reality, however, is found in Christ" (Col. 2:16–17). "For everything

God created is good, and nothing is to be rejected if it is received with thanksgiving, because it is consecrated by the word of God and prayer" (1 Tim. 4:4–5). This included food, which shows that Paul had come a long way from the days in which he would eat no pork or shellfish. While some prohibited people from eating certain foods, Paul is now declaring all foods kosher—"clean"—as Jesus had done in Mark 7:19.

In the meantime, however, the smallest piece of legislation had a meaning. They all had a purpose and consequently demanded fulfillment. But, at the moment Jesus said this in the Sermon on the Mount, these things remained unfulfilled—the specifications and all the sacrificial offerings. Jesus did not nullify these things at that moment; He still had to keep them Himself. After all, He was "born under the law" (Gal. 4:4).

THE DESTINY OF THE LAW

The Law, then, had a strategic destiny—a predestined plan. We noted in chapter one that the Law was but a parenthesis in God's plan of salvation. The Law was "added" to the promise to Abraham (Gal. 3:19), that is, it came in alongside it (Rom. 5:20). The Law existed between the times of its arrival and its accomplishment. It was temporary in God's mind and plan from the beginning. Jesus' statement therefore comes toward the end of that 1,300-year parenthesis.

> There is one thing that God the Lawgiver was determined to do from the moment He gave [the Law] to Moses: to see all the details of that Law fulfilled.

And yet there is one thing that God the Lawgiver was determined to do from the moment He gave it to Moses: to see all the details of that Law fulfilled. That purpose was so definite that even the end of the world would be delayed if this Law was not fulfilled. The very universe would be sustained if for no other reason than that the commandments of God Himself be accomplished. And that is precisely what Jesus came to do. Therefore something was more important than any other consideration: that someone come along and do what had never been done before, namely, to satisfy

26

the demands of the Law, put an end to the sacrificial system, and show why the Law came in the first place. "I am that person," Jesus was therefore saying in Matthew 5:17.

Jesus, then, was the predestined person to fulfill the Law. "I tell you the truth; until heaven and earth disappear, not the smallest letter, not the least stroke of a pen, will by any means disappear from the Law until everything is accomplished" (Matt. 5:18). Moses gave the Law but couldn't fulfill it. Joshua perpetuated the Law (Josh. 1:8) but couldn't satisfy its demands. King David loved the Law (Ps. 119:163) but broke it. The prophets upheld the Law but couldn't keep it as it required. The Levites carried out the Law, but they still came short of it. The Pharisees and Sadducees and teachers of the Law argued about it but did not have a clue as to its deeper meaning. But the very Messiah they rejected was the prophet Moses spoke of (Deut. 18:15; Acts 3:22).

THE DESTINY OF GOD'S PEOPLE

The destiny of the Law further required a predestined people. These people would not necessarily be those of the physical seed of Abraham or of Isaac or of Jacob.

> For not all who are descended from Israel are Israel. Nor because they are his descendants are they all Abraham's children. On the contrary, "It is through Isaac that your offspring will be reckoned." In other words, it is not the natural children who are God's children, but it is the children of the promise who are regarded as Abraham's offspring.
>
> —ROMANS 9:6–8

Isaiah saw it long before: "I revealed myself to those who did not ask for me; I was found by those who did not seek me. To a nation that did not call on my name, I said, 'Here am I, here am I'" (Isa. 65:1). Jesus said to the Jews of His day, "Therefore I tell you that the kingdom of God will be taken away from you and given to a people who will produce its fruit" (Matt. 21:43). The predestined people would include Jews, but also Gentiles. It would include

27

inhabitants of Jerusalem, but also Samaria. The people of God in a word are called His elect. They would be those to whom God showed sovereign mercy: "For he says to Moses, 'I will have mercy on whom I have mercy, and I will have compassion on whom I have compassion'" (Rom. 9:15). They would come from the east, the west, the north, and the south. They would constitute a "great multitude that no one could count, from every nation, tribe, people and language, standing before the throne and in front of the Lamb. They were wearing white robes and were holding palm branches in their hands" (Rev. 7:9). It would be a people who believed God as Abraham did (Gen. 15:6; Rom. 4:12), who believed the gospel long before the Law came.

You and I are invited to be among that predestined people. "For God so loved the world that he gave his one and only Son, that whoever believes in him shall not perish but have eternal life" (John 3:16). "The Spirit and the bride say, 'Come!' And let him who hears say, 'Come!' Whoever is thirsty, let him come; and whoever wishes, let him take the free gift of the water of life" (Rev. 22:17). No one need be excluded. Those who heed the invitation are given the righteousness of Jesus—as though they kept the Law themselves.

The answer to the question posed at the beginning of this chapter (Who is required to achieve all this?) is: Jesus achieved this. We are not required to accomplish what He has already achieved on our behalf. He was under the Law, but we are not. This is why Paul could say, "But if you are led by the Spirit, you are not under law" (Gal. 5:18). For being led by the Spirit leads to a righteousness that is even higher than that of the Law, as we will see in the following pages.

Chapter 3

STATUS IN THE
KINGDOM OF HEAVEN

Anyone who breaks one of the least of these
commandments and teaches others to do the
same will be called least in the kingdom of
heaven, but whoever practices and teaches these
commands will be called great in the kingdom
of heaven.

—MATTHEW 5:19

IT IS NOT likely that many, if any, of Jesus' hearers grasped
what He was actually talking about in the Sermon on the
Mount. They only knew He spoke with "authority," unlike the
teachers of the Law (Matt. 7:29). For what He had to say would not
be truly clear until after the Holy Spirit came down on the Day of
Pentecost.

A SPIRITUAL TEACHING

The Sermon on the Mount is best understood as part of Jesus'
doctrine of the Holy Spirit. The Holy Spirit is not explicitly
mentioned, however. But as God is not mentioned in the Book
of Esther—a God-centered book—so also the Sermon on the
Mount only makes sense in the light of the Holy Spirit. Although
Jesus does not explain the coming of the Spirit until the end of
His public ministry (John 14–16), the Sermon on the Mount is
inexplicable without the Spirit.

The kingdom of heaven, God's realm, is "heaven below"—the realm of the Holy Spirit. Those who are broken enter it. "Blessed are the poor in spirit, for theirs is the kingdom of heaven" (Matt. 5:3). Jesus made it clear that the kingdom "does not come with your careful observation" since it is "within you" (Luke 17:20–21). The kingdom is only experienced by the Holy Spirit indwelling a person.

This is made clearer by the unfolding of the beatitudes. The first reference to the kingdom of heaven in the Sermon on the Mount is in Matthew 5:3. It is here that one sees the connection between humility—the awareness of spiritual bankruptcy—and the entrance into the kingdom.

We enter the kingdom of heaven by being born again (John 3:3). It is what happens to us when we pray, "God, have mercy on me, a sinner" (Luke 18:13). To ask for mercy requires humility. It means we have no power to bargain with God. For when one asks for mercy one knows it can be given or withheld, and justice will be done either way. God can be "just" by forgiving us (1 John 1:9) because His justice was satisfied by Christ's death. The Greek that translates "have mercy" in Luke 18:13 really means "be propitiated," that is, look on the "mercy seat" where the blood is sprinkled. This is a direct reference to the Day of Atonement when the high priest atoned with blood for the sins of the people. Thus when we enter the kingdom of heaven, we are humbly conscious of God's graciousness to us.

Never forget that a kingdom presupposes a monarch—a king or a queen. When one is invited into the presence of a monarch it is a gracious invitation. Only a sovereign has the right to invite who comes into his or her presence. God is sovereign. He has the right to invite who comes into His presence. It is the highest privilege known to a human being. What is more startling is that God wants to live in us! The kingdom of heaven therefore means that God, who was ever the King of His people Israel, wants to indwell the hearts of His people. This is done by the Spirit. To the extent that the Holy Spirit is utterly Himself, the awareness of His place and presence is realized. When the Spirit is Himself it means He is ungrieved and unquenched.

Before proceeding any further, I want to explain what I mean by the Holy Spirit being Himself. We all know the expression, "Make yourself at home." People say that to us to make us feel comfortable and at ease. But few of us really do that in another's house. If I were totally myself when I came to your home I would, first of all, bring my dressing gown and, second, take off my shoes. If I came to your carefully prepared table in my dressing gown and slippers, it would probably be you who was ill at ease, not me! But I would be making myself at home!

> If the Holy Spirit were completely withdrawn from the church today, 90 percent of the work of the church would go on as if nothing had happened.

I have a feeling that if the Holy Spirit were utterly Himself in our churches, it would be we who were ill at ease! We aren't prepared for what He is really like. We may sing the old hymn "Have Thine Own Way, Lord," but were the Lord to have His own way in us it would turn everything upside-down! This is why I believe it is true that if the Holy Spirit were completely withdrawn from the church today, 90 percent of the work of the church would go on as if nothing had happened.

The reason is this. The Holy Spirit is a person—and a very sensitive person at that. He can be grieved (Eph. 4:30), which means He gets His feelings hurt. And He can be quenched (1 Thess. 5:19), which means what He is doing can in some sense be stopped. We grieve Him by bitterness and conduct that dishonors His name. We quench Him by fear and unbelief.

The four Gospels depict the Holy Spirit as a dove. The dove is a very shy bird, possibly the most sensitive bird in the world. You may feed the pigeons in London's Trafalgar Square, but you will never get a dove to perch upon your shoulder! And yet the Holy Spirit is said to have come down on Jesus like a dove when He was baptized (Matt. 3:16; Mark 1:10; Luke 3:22). John the Baptist was assured that Jesus was the one he had been waiting for because of the dove that came to Jesus and remained. "I would not have known him, except that the one who sent me to baptize with water told me, 'The man on whom you see the Spirit come down and remain is he who will baptize with the Holy Spirit' (John 1:33). The dove remained on Jesus. I have to admit that the dove does

31

not remain very long on me. I may feel a touch of the dove on me—so peaceful and joyous—only to notice He has unobtrusively fluttered away. Whether it be because of bitterness, an unguarded comment, or listening to malicious gossip—I only know that the sweet presence of the Spirit does not remain long with me. But it remained on Jesus.

ADJUSTING TO THE SPIRIT

I heard of a couple, broken and bruised, who took a sabbatical in Israel. They rented a house near Jerusalem—just to rest and recuperate. Soon after they arrived they noticed that a dove had come to live in the eaves of their house. They were thrilled. But every time a door was slammed they noticed that the dove flew away and would not return for hours. The man said to his wife, "Have you noticed the dove that has come to live in our roof?"

"Yes," she said.

"How do you feel about the dove?" he asked her.

"I feel it is almost a sign from the Lord—it is wonderful," she replied.

"Have you noticed that every time we slam a door, the dove flies away?" he then asked her.

"Yes," she replied, "and it makes me sad."

He then concluded: "Either the dove adjusts to us, or we adjust to the dove."

When we want the anointing of the Holy Spirit to remain on us, we must adjust to the dove. He is easily grieved. It does not take a lot to make Him move away. When we grieve the Spirit it does not mean we have lost our salvation. "And do not grieve the Holy Spirit of God, with whom you were sealed for the day of redemption" (Eph. 4:30). Nothing can be clearer than that. But it does mean we lose joy, peace, presence of mind, and clear thinking. The issue is, simply, whether or not He is ungrieved. That way He stays around.

My point is this. When the Holy Spirit is ungrieved and unquenched, He is Himself. He does and acts as He really wants to do and act. He carries on unhindered. What implications this has for our church services is not something I can go into in this book, but it certainly has relevance for each of us in our personal lives, which is one of the main points of this book. If the Holy Spirit is ungrieved and unquenched in me, I will manifest the beatitudes (for one thing) and carry out the Ten Commandments in a manner never dreamed of by the Pharisees and scribes. The key is the Holy Spirit, for the kingdom of heaven is His realm. When I am in the kingdom I am in the realm of the Spirit.

The two references to the kingdom of heaven in Matthew 5:19 indicate rank or status in the kingdom. For example, there is the possibility of being the "least" and also of being "great." In this chapter we shall attempt to understand precisely what this means and why Jesus used such language with reference to the Law.

JESUS' TEACHING ON THE LAW

We saw in the previous chapter that the whole of the Law—not just the Ten Commandments but even the minute specifications of the Law—must be fulfilled. The immediate question that now arises is, to what do "the least of these commandments" of Matthew 5:19 refer? To the Law (and those two thousand verses of legislation)? Or does Jesus refer to what He will shortly say as He proceeds in the Sermon on the Mount ("You have heard...but I tell you")? Some are of the opinion that Jesus is preparing His hearers for what will shortly be coming up, namely, His own treatment of the various commandments in Matthew 5:21–48.

But what is the most natural way of taking Jesus' words? Having just said, "I tell you the truth, until heaven and earth disappear, not the smallest letter, not the least stroke of a pen, will by any means disappear from the Law until everything is accomplished" (Matt. 5:18), then adding, "Anyone who breaks one of the least of these commands," the natural way of taking this would be to say that it seems to refer to what Jesus had just said. For "least stroke of the pen" surely applies to "the least of these commands." Matthew 5:19 is therefore elaborating on verse 18 and means exactly what it says with reference to keeping all the commands of the Law—even those that refer to agriculture, dress, and diet, which Jesus kept.

Matthew 5:19 is not an easy verse to understand, but it is

one we must nonetheless grasp. The main question obviously is this: if Jesus Himself fulfilled the Law, do we today have to keep the minutiae of the Law? No, which I will make clear below. By minutiae of the Law I refer to such passages as:

> Three times a year you are to celebrate a festival to me.
>
> —EXODUS 23:14

> Do not offer the blood of a sacrifice to me along with anything containing yeast. The fat of my festival offerings must not be kept until morning. Bring the best of the first-fruits of your soil to the house of the LORD your God. Do not cook a young goat in its mother's milk.
>
> —EXODUS 23:18–19

> Do not wear clothing woven of two kinds of material.
>
> —LEVITICUS 19:19

> Do not cut the hair at the sides of your head or clip off the edges of your beard.
>
> —LEVITICUS 19:27

> Of all the creatures living in the water, you may eat any that has fins and scales. But anything that does not have fins and scales you may not eat; for you it is unclean.
>
> —DEUTERONOMY 14:9–10

One could go on and on in quoting verses that had relevance then but not for us today. And yet if Matthew 5:19 refers to verse 18, why did Jesus appear to relax particular requirements of the Law and seem to teach others to do so when, for example, He pronounced all foods "clean" (Mark 7:19) even before He fulfilled the Law? Not only that; Jesus spoke against divorce (Matt. 5:32; 19:9), but the Law allowed divorce (Deut. 24:1–4). Jesus spoke against taking of oaths (Matt. 5:34), but the Law even demanded them (Num. 30:1–2). Matthew 5:18 refers to the minutiae of the Law, and Matthew 5:19—referring to such—says one must not break any of them.

The second question follows, therefore, how do we reconcile

Jesus' "relaxing" of the Law (as in Mark 7:19) with His own words, "Anyone who breaks one of the least of these commandments and teaches others to do the same will be called least in the kingdom of heaven, but whoever practices and teaches these commands will be called great in the kingdom of heaven" (Matt. 5:19)? The answer is that He was clearly moving in the direction of relaxing the minutiae but nonetheless required all the commands to be honored at the time.

A third question we must ask is, if the kingdom of heaven is the realm of the unquenched Spirit, does one get into the kingdom by keeping the "least" commands? If so, surely the Pharisees and the teachers of the Law were already in it! The answer is, His followers would be honored for their conscientiousness and care to obey as they patiently waited for the kingdom to be unfolded. God would not forget their careful obedience.

A fourth question is, did Jesus merely want to show that He Himself upholds the Law to the hilt since He said He hadn't come to abolish but to fulfill it? As we will see, it is far more serious than that; He was under a mandate to fulfill the Law utterly and totally.

It must be stated yet again at this point that Jesus' words in the Sermon on the Mount, especially Matthew 5:18, were almost certainly not understood by His hearers at the time. For they could hardly be understood until after the Holy Spirit came down on the Day of Pentecost. His disciples must therefore have been puzzled by what a statement like this meant. In Matthew 5:19 Jesus gives no hint at all of relaxing the Law—and yet He Himself would be bringing changes in what obedience means in the kingdom of heaven. After all, how could there be a greater loyalty to the written Scriptures than what was shown by the teachers of the Law and the Pharisees?

THE KINGDOM OF HEAVEN

The only way forward is to see the kingdom of heaven from two points of view: the pre-Pentecostal period and the post-Pentecostal era. The former—the pre-Pentecostal period—began with John the Baptist (Matt. 11:12; Luke 16:16). Both John and Jesus proclaimed the good news of the kingdom of heaven (Matt. 3:1–2; 4:17, 23). Jesus' words in Matthew 5:19, it must be remembered, were uttered at a time when the Law was still unfulfilled. This was therefore still in the pre-Pentecostal period. In Matthew 5:17 Jesus promised to fulfill the Law; in verse 18 He showed that He realized His work was clearly cut out for Him. In Matthew 5:19 He shows what the responsibility of every one of His followers was at that time.

If we keep in mind that the Law was still unfulfilled—though Jesus was on the scene—Matthew 5:19 makes complete sense. The parenthesis to which I referred in chapter one was not yet closed. As I said, Jesus had perhaps two years or more left before He finally fulfilled the Law. In the meantime, then, not only was He going to keep it, He urged His followers to do the same. So until that Law was fulfilled these two things followed: first, Jesus Himself would keep it, and second, His disciples must keep it as well. "Anyone who breaks one of the least of these commandments and teaches others to do the same will be called least in the kingdom of heaven, but whoever practices and teaches these commands will be called great in the kingdom of heaven" (Matt. 5:19). It follows from these words, then, that people could be in the kingdom of heaven then. In other words, being in the kingdom of heaven need not await either Jesus' death or the coming of the Spirit on the Day of Pentecost.

But how could one enter the kingdom of heaven, if this is the realm of the Spirit, before the Holy Spirit fell at Pentecost? The answer is: by obedience to Jesus at the time. Although people did not fully grasp all the implications of His teaching, they still had the choice to receive Him or reject Him. If they received Him, they were going to receive the benefit of the Spirit coming in great power later. After all, "Whoever can be trusted with very little can also be trusted with much, and whoever is dishonest with very little will also be dishonest with much" (Luke 16:10). To the extent people were faithful to what Jesus said to them then, to that extent they would enjoy what would be clearer later. In a word: Jesus' followers—those who embraced Him and His words—were in the kingdom of heaven then and there.

In this pre-Pentecostal period, which, I suspect, would last another two years or so, anyone who broke "one of the least commandments" would be regarded "least" in the kingdom. Jesus did not say they could not be "in" it; He said that they would be regarded "least" in it if they broke any of the least commandments at the time and if they taught others to do so. In making a statement like this He sent an even stronger signal to those revolutionaries who hoped Jesus would do away with Mosaic legislation entirely. They would not have been pleased. Also, by saying what He did in verse 19, in one stroke He kept the Pharisees and teachers of the Law from any undue criticism. For one thing, they could never accuse Him of antinomianism (which means doing away with the Law). Not that Jesus was sensitive to such a criticism—as some today might be, but He certainly did not give His critics a chance to exploit any opportunity at this stage.

Jesus was therefore saying to all who heard Him that they must literally keep the whole of the Mosaic Law until He Himself fulfilled it. That meant they had to keep the Sabbath, the feasts, the detailed specifications—and the sacrifices were to be offered. There would be no relaxing of the Law, according to Matthew 5:19. For Jesus was still in the process of fulfilling the Law. Moreover, all who followed Him must do the same—right to the end. This is why Jesus still kept the Passover with His disciples on the night before the crucifixion. "On the first day of the Feast of Unleavened Bread, the disciples came to Jesus and asked, 'Where do you want us to make preparations for you to eat the Passover?'" (Matt. 26:17). These words show that they took for granted that they and Jesus would be observing Passover. It did not cross their minds to think in any other manner. For the Mosaic Law was not nullified for them or, for that matter, for anyone who wanted to be of stature in the kingdom of heaven. All of Jesus' followers must go all the way with the Law until it was fulfilled.

To put it another way, Jesus did not give a hint that, by His own fulfilling the Law, He would even fulfill the Passover. He Himself would ultimately be "our Passover lamb" (1 Cor. 5:7), but Jesus kept the Passover nonetheless. Never once did Jesus say to a handful of His followers, "Look, My friends, do not worry about those small details of the Law, not to mention the sacrifices, for I am going to take care of those for you—do not worry about them any more." No. He Himself kept the whole of the Law, and He required all of His followers, if they wanted to have great stature in the kingdom, to do the same thing.

We must also keep in mind that at the time Jesus uttered these words His followers did not conceive of such a thing as a post-Pentecostal era. At this stage, they still believed He would overthrow Rome! As we have seen already, they still thought of the kingdom in terms of visibility and political relevance. Even after Jesus died they did not know at first that the Law had now been fulfilled. They did not even understand His death. After His resurrection, just before His unexpected ascension, they asked Him, "Lord, are you at this time going to restore the kingdom to Israel?" (Acts 1:6). For they did not have a clue even at this stage what fulfilling the Law meant and that Jesus had done it by His death on the cross. All of this did not come home to them until after the Holy Spirit came down at Pentecost (Acts 2:1–36).

It was after the coming of the Spirit, then, that the disciples realized (and even then in stages) that Christ fulfilled the Law by His sinless life and sacrificial death and that Christ continued to fulfill the Law through His disciples by the power of the Holy Spirit. The early church developed in understanding as they were forced to reflect on issues that arose. They were helped by the major clarification provided by Paul. Peter was helped by seeing how the Holy Spirit fell on Cornelius—a Gentile (Acts 10). But it was Paul who seemed to be the first to grasp fully how Christ's death fulfilled the Law. He saw that the righteousness of the Law continued by life in the Spirit; the minutiae of the Law ceased to be relevant. For after the Spirit came there was a simultaneous continuity and discontinuity. The morality of the Law continued; the minutiae of the Law discontinued. Indeed, the righteousness of the Law would exceed any level of righteousness ever conceived! It would be through the power of the Holy Spirit (Rom. 8:4).

We may be reminded ourselves that we today are in that post-Pentecostal era of the kingdom of heaven. Christ was our substitute; He kept the whole of the Law perfectly. He is our satisfaction before God (Isa. 53:6; 2 Cor. 5:21) and our substitutionary sanctification (1 Cor. 1:30). That means that Jesus who was perfectly sinless and holy was our substitute before God. He is, on our behalf, our very sanctification. It is perfect and unimprovable. Thank

God for that! But our own sanctification (1 Thess. 4:3), though progressive, is produced by the power of the Holy Spirit. It is a paradox—contradictory but true: Christ is our sanctification, but we nonetheless exhibit a sanctification that people see and that honors God. That is why Jesus said, "In the same way, let your light shine before men, that they may see your good deeds and praise your Father in heaven" (Matt. 5:16).

So how did one get into the kingdom of heaven before the Day of Pentecost and before Jesus even died on the cross? The answer is, by receiving Jesus then and there (John 1:12). All they needed to do was to come to Him. "Come to me, all you who are weary and burdened, and I will give you rest" (Matt. 11:28). Those who believed Him entered the kingdom. Those who rejected Him did not get in it at all—no matter how respectful they were of the Law. As for those who believed and followed Jesus, some may well have been more zealous than others. Those who kept the commands at that stage were to be called "great" in the kingdom.

THE LEAST AND THE GREATEST

This brings us to the aforementioned rank or status in the kingdom, a rather new concept that Jesus introduced in Matthew 5:19. There are apparently levels of stature, or prestige, in the kingdom. Some would be regarded "least" by breaking one of the least of the commands of the Mosaic Law and by teaching others to do the same. On the other hand, those who kept and taught such commands would be esteemed "great" in the kingdom of heaven. It is obvious from these words that some commandments are greater, or more important, than others. Therefore it follows, according to Jesus, that the subjects of the kingdom have varying degrees of stature, or status, and are affirmed according to their observance of all the commandments. It is a further affirmation of "every jot and tittle" of the Law, as the King James Version puts it; God will reward all those in the kingdom who take the Mosaic Law seriously up until the time it is finally fulfilled.

Jesus had already introduced the idea of "reward" in the beatitudes when He said, "Rejoice and be glad, because great is your reward in heaven, for in the same way they persecuted the prophets who were before you" (Matt. 5:12). Later on in Matthew's Gospel He even said:

> Anyone who receives a prophet because he is a prophet will receive a prophet's reward, and anyone who receives a righteous man because he is a righteous man will receive a righteous man's reward. And if anyone gives even a cup of cold water to one of these little ones because he is my disciple, I tell you the truth, he will certainly not lose his reward.
>
> —MATTHEW 10:41–42

In this kind of teaching, which seems strange to some Christians who carry the doctrines of grace to such an extent that they fear that a concept of works will somehow creep into the picture, Jesus actually appeals to our self-esteem. And yet this should not really surprise us. God has always done this, even appealing to our self-interest. The first words God uttered to Abraham included the promise, "I will make your name great" (Gen. 12:2), and God certainly did that.

When Jesus therefore said that keeping God's commands would mean being called "great," He was referring to one's rank—"great" as opposed to being "least"—and reputation. Reputation then meant both how God would regard such people and how others, too, would regard them. They would be called great.

But these words were applicable to the pre-Pentecostal period—before the Law was fulfilled by Jesus.

The question follows, would this teaching not have implications for those in the kingdom in the post-Pentecostal era as well? The answer is surely, yes. First of all, those who were in the kingdom (by receiving Jesus) and who took the least of the commands seriously—affirming the Law as Jesus did—would undoubtedly be remembered after the coming of the Spirit. In other words, those who took the greatest care to observe the minute specifications of the Law were earmarked for greatness later on. Keeping the minutiae of the Law was possibly good training for the future. Those who took such care would probably be the ones who made sure they did not grieve the Spirit later on—by the smallest things.

Never forget that Jesus said, "Whoever can be trusted with very little can also be trusted with much, and whoever is dishonest with very little will also be dishonest with much" (Luke 16:10). I doubt not, then, that those who took Jesus' words very seriously were singled out by God after the Spirit came down and were trusted with a greater responsibility and anointing. The disciples were thus destined for greatness after Pentecost, and they are almost certainly among those whose names are mentioned in the Book of Acts. But many others not mentioned in Acts will be honored at the judgment seat of Christ: "For we must all appear before the judgment seat of Christ, that each one may receive what is due to him for the things done while in the body, whether good or bad" (2 Cor. 5:10).

THE REQUIREMENTS OF THE SPIRIT

If I may return to a previous question, if Jesus would be relaxing certain requirements and yet maintaining what He said in Matthew 5:19, what was truly going on? As we have seen, He clearly relaxed some requirements by calling all foods kosher; He also prohibited swearing of oaths. So He threw out hints along the way as to what the commandments of the kingdom would be like. He clearly interpreted, embellished, and outclassed all the commandments at the end of the day. So what was going on? I can only conclude that Jesus was clearly moving in a direction in which the Law would be transcended; not disregarded but outclassed, as Dr. Michael Eaton puts it.

When Jesus later began using language in the Sermon on the Mount, "You have heard...but I tell you" (Matt. 5:21–44), He was not upholding the minutiae of the Law but the spiritual morality of the Ten Commandments. The Sermon on the Mount would not only be part of Jesus' teaching of the Spirit but also the way the Holy Spirit interprets the Ten Commandments. His commands beginning with "But I tell you" outstrip and outclass the equivalent commands in the Law. The irony is that, whereas Jesus rocked the boat more than any other figure in human history, at the same time He held fast to the Law His Father gave to Moses and Israel. Matthew 5:19 shows He did not rock the boat on that matter and would not allow His followers to do so. In taking this stand He did not give the Pharisees or teachers of the Law an inch by which they could justly challenge Him. He adhered carefully to the word and insisted that His followers do the same. They would even be rewarded for so doing.

Finally, would there be "least" commands in the post-Pentecostal era? Yes. It is always true that "little foxes" ruin the vineyards (Song of Sol. 2:15), and those who are not conscientious in their walk with Christ will inevitably have a lot to answer for. For example, I have long been impressed by David's being smitten by his conscience merely for cutting off a piece of Saul's robe (1 Sam. 24:5). This could be seen as a small thing. Many would want to say, surely, that is being too conscientious. But if one took that same care in not grieving the Holy Spirit—by avoiding any trace of bitterness—I would have thought the reward would be great. Developing a hypersensitivity to the Holy Spirit pays great dividends.

There is therefore a principle that emerges from Matthew 5:19. Although the minutiae of the Law are no longer required of Jesus' followers, since He nailed them to the cross (Col. 2:14), there are, nonetheless, matters that pertain to conscientious Christian living that some might think as small as David's being convicted by cutting off a piece of Saul's robe. It depends on the degree we are prepared to adjust to the dove—the Spirit. If we are to develop a hypersensitivity to the Spirit it will almost certainly come as a result of keeping the smallest details of kingdom living. Jesus develops such in Matthew 5:21–48.

I can never forget something Dr. Martyn Lloyd-Jones taught me in those days when I visited him at his home in Ealing every Thursday for two years. "The devil must be resisted in detail," he would say. This meant dealing with the smallest thing. For example, any negative thought that the devil would put in one's mind must be resisted—then and there—or one would get no victory later on. Likewise, in following the Holy Spirit, one must take on board the smallest thing that the Holy Spirit brings to your attention. If we are faithful in the "least" thing, we will be faithful in the greater thing (Luke 16:10). Those who develop this conscientiousness before God will be regarded as "great" in the kingdom. Not by people, but by God. It is He who bestows status in the realm of the Spirit.

Chapter 4

THE LAW OUTCLASSED

For I tell you that unless your righteousness surpasses that of the Pharisees and the teachers of the law, you will certainly not enter the kingdom of heaven.

—MATTHEW 5:20

I N THIS VERSE Jesus further sets the stage for His understanding of the righteousness of the Law. He wants to show the kind of righteousness that must characterize those who enter the kingdom of heaven. By lumping two groups together—the teachers of the Law and the Pharisees—Jesus also gives a picture of superficial righteousness.

SCRIBES AND PHARISEES

Who were the teachers of the Law, or "scribes" as the King James Version calls them? They were seen as the ultimate authorities when it came to interpreting the Law. Their hero was Ezra, a teacher "well versed in the Law of Moses" (Ezra 7:6). The scribes became an elitist group. They would have been perhaps regarded as professional interpreters. They were also copyists, having the grave responsibility of copying the Old Testament without any error. They not only interpreted Israel's sacred literature; they gathered

43

it and were probably among those who had selected and fixed the Old Testament canon. They belonged to the *Hassidim*—"pious." They had undoubted authority in people's eyes. Jesus referred to it but took little notice of the men themselves, except to put them into perspective. "The teachers of the law and the Pharisees sit in Moses' seat. So you must obey them and do everything they tell you. But do not do what they do, for they do not practice what they preach" (Matt. 23:2–3).

Who were the Pharisees? They were virtually a political party in Jesus' day and were very influential. Their hero was also Ezra, and all they believed centered on the Law. The name "Pharisee" seems to have been derived from two things:

1. Being separationists: being separate from the people but also from the priestly interpretation of the Law

2. Regarding themselves as interpreters, they fancied that they were superior interpreters of the Law.

They were very legalistic and known for their rigorous interpretation as well as strict accuracy and scrupulous adherence to these interpretations. They were said to build a fence around the Law with their embellishments to the Law, this fence being their own interpretation and traditions. They held to what was called "the tradition of the elders" (Mark 7:3).

The Pharisees and the scribes were often seen together, and, as I said, Jesus merely lumped them together. Some teachers of the Law were also Pharisees (Mark 2:16). They loved tradition (Matt. 15:3–4), did not really practice what they preached (Matt. 23:3), and had no objectivity about themselves. For example, they built the tombs of the prophets and thought they were indeed a cut above those who killed the prophets. Jesus pointed out, "You build tombs for the prophets and decorate the graves of the righteous. And you say, 'If we had lived in the days of our forefathers, we would not have taken part with them in shedding the blood of the prophets'" (Matt. 23:29–30). They did not conceive that they were in fact the successors of those who killed the prophets (vv. 31–32). They were strict tithers, but the single motivation for their righteousness was to be seen by men; moreover, they had no concept of inward sin (Luke 18:11–12). Jesus called them snakes and told them they were on the road to hell (Matt. 23:33). Jesus even held them responsible for the way the whole nation would be judged (vv. 35–36).

I do not mean to be unfair, but it seems to me that there are people today who think they are the successors to the disciples of Jesus in the early church who are rather successors to the Pharisees instead. Now it is easy to brand anybody a "Pharisee" who may not agree with our own point of view, so we must be careful. For we can all become Pharisees before we know it and thus be like them before we know it. Judging is wrong and God will not bend the rules for any of us (Matt. 7:1–2). And yet if people opt for being hypersensitive to what threatens their party line rather than being hypersensitive to the Spirit, such people unwittingly betray whose succession they really uphold. The Pharisees were champions of the Law but tended to hate almost everything Jesus stood for. Even with all its power—like that of the Pharisees joining forces with the teachers of the Law—God can hold a church or a nation responsible and put such under His wrathful judgment as He has done before.

The Pharisees in particular criticized Jesus for healing on the Sabbath (Matt. 12:9–14). They seemed to live to trap Jesus by His words (Matt. 22:15). They accused Jesus of casting out devils by Beelzebub the prince of devils (Matt. 12:24). They criticized Jesus' followers for being sinners (Matt. 9:11). The teachers of the Law conspired to kill Jesus (Mark 11:18) and accused Jesus before Herod (Luke 23:10). They were always challenging Jesus' authority (Matt. 21:23).

Almost certainly nobody ever dared to stand up either to the Pharisees or to the teachers of the Law. These men felt that the Law was theirs; that they had a monopoly, or franchise, on the correct interpretation of the Law. They saw themselves as successors not only to Ezra but also to Moses. If God were going to do anything in Israel, it would surely come through them; they assumed that they would be the first to be notified! For they thought of themselves as the sole upholders of the Scriptures.

Jesus saw right through them. For one thing, they were not even in what He called the kingdom of heaven. In other words, not only were they not the "least" in the kingdom, they were not even in it at all. In fact, said Jesus, they actually kept people from entering it. "Woe to you, teachers of the law and Pharisees, you hypocrites! You shut the kingdom of heaven in men's faces. You yourselves do not enter, nor will you let those enter who are trying to" (Matt. 23:13). Their converts were doubly the sons of hell (v. 15).

THE RIGHTEOUSNESS OF THE KINGDOM

Imagine the stunned silence that must have swept over the people when Jesus said, "For I tell you that unless your righteousness surpasses that of the Pharisees and the teachers of the law, you will certainly not enter the kingdom of heaven" (Matt. 5:20). Nobody had ever talked like this before. The common people in those days took for granted that the Pharisees and the teachers of the Law were righteous men. If anyone got into the kingdom of heaven, they did.

This reminds me of an old song—quite ludicrous—that was introduced in the Deep South in the United States a few years ago. It talks about various good works one does to ensure getting to heaven at the end of the day, including reading the Bible! Those who write such—I knew some of them—were sincere but seriously misguided. And it suggests the very feeling the Pharisees of Jesus' day had about themselves.

> The greatest freedom in the world is having nothing to prove. Where the Spirit is, there is liberty (2 Cor. 3:17). This means a wonderful sense of fearlessness.

In any case, no ordinary Jew in those days ever dreamed that he or she could even equal the righteousness of the teachers of the Law or the Pharisees. After all, their standard of righteous living was beyond reproach. Their adherence to the Law was unquestioned. No ordinary person in Israel dreamed of being so pious. These citizens of Israel felt they were outstripped by the Pharisees and teachers of the Law. Can you therefore picture the sobered expressions on people's faces—the shocked atmosphere—when Jesus said the words of Matthew 5:20? *Surpass their righteousness? We can't even come up to their level*, the people must have thought. *How can we surpass the righteousness of the scribes and Pharisees?* But Jesus stuck to His guns.

How, then, can righteousness surpass—exceed, or go beyond— righteousness such as theirs? The answer is quite simple. Their righteousness was only an external righteousness. Jesus later said:

> Woe to you, teachers of the law and Pharisees, you hypocrites! You clean the outside of the cup and dish, but inside they are full of greed and self-indulgence. Blind Pharisee! First clean the inside of the cup and dish, and then the outside also will be clean.
>
> —MATTHEW 23:25–26

It did not reach their hearts. It was all for show.

> Everything they do is done for men to see: They make their phylacteries wide and the tassels on their garments long; they love the place of honor at banquets and the most important seats in the synagogues; they love to be greeted in the marketplaces and to have men call them "Rabbi."
>
> —MATTHEW 23:5–7

It was entirely for the praise of men. They loved to pray "standing in the synagogues and on the street corners to be seen by men" (Matt. 6:5). They fasted but did so to "show men they are fasting" (v. 16). "He said to them, 'You are the ones who justify yourselves in the eyes of men, but God knows your hearts. What is highly valued among men is detestable in God's sight'" (Luke 16:15).

Jesus was so utterly unafraid of people like this. We must be like this. The greatest freedom in the world is having nothing to prove. Where the Spirit is, there is liberty (2 Cor. 3:17). This means a wonderful sense of fearlessness. Fearlessness is more than courage. One can be courageous but inwardly scared! True fearlessness is being utterly at ease, as if you were in your living room in slippers with your feet propped up. It is a calmness of spirit that inwardly laughs at critics who are motivated by fear. Jesus showed this when He stood in silence before Herod, who wanted to see a miracle

(Luke 23:8–9). But Jesus had nothing to prove! Yet the people were intimidated by the Pharisees. Even some leaders were in fear of them. "Yet at the same time many even among the leaders believed in him. But because of the Pharisees they would not confess their faith for fear they would be put out of the synagogue" (John 12:42). Jesus now sends a signal to the most insignificant Jew in Israel, the most common worshiper. The frail Israelite who never thought he would add up to a row of beans is now affirmed: he or she could not only have a personal righteousness but a righteousness that surpasses the piety of these "professionals." This is partly what Jesus meant by the words, "So the last will be first, and the first will be last" (Matt. 20:16).

How then is it possible for a person—then as well as now—to have a righteousness that is superior to that of a Pharisee or teacher of the Law? There are several answers. To begin with, although this is not really what Jesus is referring to, anyone in the kingdom—even if he or she is amongst the "least"—has a righteousness not their own. Paul the Apostle called it an "imputed" righteousness (Rom. 4:1–25, KJV). This means righteousness put to one's credit by virtue of faith. This is at the very heart of the gospel, though, as I said, it is not what Jesus means in this instance. And yet it is absolutely true: once a person transfers the trust that he or she once had in their own good works and now trusts Christ's blood, the very righteousness of Jesus is simultaneously transferred to them. And no scribe or Pharisee could even begin to come up to that standard! The very righteousness of Jesus who fulfilled the Law is put to our credit. "However, to the man who does not work but trusts God who justifies the wicked, his faith is credited as righteousness" (Rom. 4:5). This is what I meant in the previous chapter by talking of Christ being our sanctification (1 Cor. 1:30).

However, I repeat: that is not what Jesus actually means by our righteousness surpassing that of the Pharisees. Righteousness is actually imputed to us of course, and that obviously goes beyond the righteousness of the Pharisees and teachers of the Law. But Jesus mainly meant an internal righteousness. It is implanted (James 1:21). It is imparted by the Holy Spirit (1 Thess. 1:5; 2:13). It is what Jeremiah prophesied:

"It will not be like the covenant
    I made with their forefathers
when I took them by the hand
    to lead them out of Egypt,
because they broke my covenant,
    though I was a husband to them,"
declares the LORD.
—JEREMIAH 31:32 (SEE ALSO HEBREWS 8:10–12)

It is a righteousness that touches the whole person. Not just in public but in private; not just before men but before God. It touches the body.

Therefore, I urge you, brothers, in view of God's mercy, to offer your bodies as living sacrifices, holy and pleasing to God—this is your spiritual act of worship.
—ROMANS 12:1

It touches the mind, or spirit.

Do not conform any longer to the pattern of this world, but be transformed by the renewing of your mind. Then you will be able to test and approve what God's will is—his good, pleasing and perfect will.
—ROMANS 12:2

It gives an ever-deepening sense of sin and an ever-increasing consciousness of the Holy Spirit.

It is the result of what I referred to earlier as resisting the devil "in detail" and taking on board what the Spirit shows us. As we walk in the light (1 John 1:7) we become more aware of sin in us (1 John 1:8), like peeling the layers of an onion. So often I will say, "Lord, why have You not shown this about myself before?" It can be so embarrassing—even more so if a close friend says, "I always knew you had that fault!" Others can see defects in us that the Holy Spirit seems to take years to uncover. Why so long? Probably because of our stubbornness and therefore not being ready to listen. But God is patient. And yet as I do walk in the light not only do I begin to see new levels of sin and fresh areas of obedience, but best of all, I also discover that it coheres with the very way Jesus applied the Law in the Sermon on the Mount! So what one discovers is nothing new; it just takes time for us to see ourselves with objectivity.

The Law, perfect though it was, did not envisage the kind of righteousness Jesus had in mind. It was given as a temporary measure—the parenthesis to which I have repeatedly referred—to restrain sin, as we will see further below. But it was not designed to produce the kind of righteousness Jesus was about to describe. If the Law was capable of this kind of righteousness, surely the Pharisees and teachers of the Law would have attained to it already. But it did not even produce a conviction of inward sin in them, much less bring about the internal righteousness Jesus was preparing to describe.

It was at this point that Jesus began a series of interpretations of the Law by the Spirit that was characterized by these words: "You have heard that it was said…but I tell you" (Matt. 5:21–22, 27–28, 31–32, 33–34, 38–39, 43–44). Jesus did not deal with each of the Ten Commandments. We may well wish He had. But He has given us enough in the Sermon on the Mount so that one can go back to the Ten Commandments and fairly accurately grasp the way Jesus would have understood each of them.

We now turn to the Ten Commandments. We shall attempt to interpret them in the light of the gospel and the spirit in which Jesus interpreted them. The gospel has priority over the Law.

The Holy Spirit applies the gospel through which we today are meant to understand the Ten Commandments.

50

Chapter 5

THE REASON FOR
THE TEN COMMANDMENTS

The LORD wrote on these tablets what he had
written before, the Ten Commandments he had
proclaimed to you on the mountain, out of the
fire, on the day of the assembly.

—DEUTERONOMY 10:4

ONE OF THE first films I ever saw was Cecil B. DeMille's
production of *The Ten Commandments*. Going to the cinema
was forbidden by my old denomination. But even my dad
eventually slipped into a cinema (praying that the devil wouldn't
cause anybody to see him) to see *The Ten Commandments*.

A few years later, shortly after I came to Westminster Chapel,
I was privileged to meet Charlton Heston, the man who played
Moses in *The Ten Commandments*. But I couldn't help wondering
if this is the closest some people will ever get to Moses or the Ten
Commandments. I wished I would have asked Mr. Heston whether
playing the role had any impact on his own life. I do fear that
millions have seen this film without their lives being affected.

The truth is, many know the Ten Commandments backward
and forward without their having much impact. Also, far more
could not even name them. Most people only vaguely know about
the seventh commandment: "You shall not commit adultery."
This one, along with the fourth commandment ("Remember the

Sabbath day by keeping it holy"), seemed to matter most to the Pharisees of Jesus' day. They were hardly prepared, moreover, for Jesus' treatment of the sixth commandment ("You shall not murder"), His teaching that hate was murder in the heart.

It is an irony to be remembered that Moses himself was a murderer. Years before he even dreamed of such a set of principles, he himself murdered an Egyptian to prove to the Israelites that he was one of them (Exod. 2:11–13). It is no small comfort to know that if God could use a murderer to write these laws He can use any of us to preach them. God is gracious.

Moses' crime led him to the Sinai desert to escape the wrath of both the Egyptians and the Israelites. It was God's way of keeping him from being successful prematurely. Dr. Martyn Lloyd-Jones once said to me, "The worst thing that can happen to a man is to be successful before he is ready." Success often goes to a person's head. One takes himself too seriously. He becomes unteachable. You can always tell a successful person, but you can't tell him or her much. King Saul, Israel's first king, took himself too seriously. He wouldn't listen to Samuel (1 Sam. 13, 15). Saul succeeded too soon. God raised up David but ensured that David would not succeed until he was ready. After being anointed and experiencing the Spirit in power (1 Sam. 16:13), it would be another twenty years before David became king. Moses needed forty years of preparation before he could be trusted to be a leader of the children of Israel. Charles Spurgeon once said that if he knew he had twenty-five years left to live, he would spend twenty of them in preparation. But one day Moses was ready.

The man who saw more of the miraculous—"signs and wonders"—than anybody in the Old Testament was the same person who delivered the strongest word from God. Long before Moses spoke the Law from Sinai he saw the Holy Spirit move in an extraordinary manner. It began with the burning bush (Exod. 3:2). It continued with his staff being turned into a serpent (Exod. 4:3). Then came the ten plagues in Egypt, culminating in the Passover and the Israelites walking across the Red Sea on dry ground (Exod. 7–14). The miraculous included the manna in the desert (Exod. 16) and the Lord descending on Sinai in fire (Exod. 19). Then came the strangest and most terrifying word God had given to anybody up to that time—the Ten Commandments (Exod. 20). Today the church needs the combination of the miraculous and the awesome—we may call it the Word and the Spirit. The Word and Spirit certainly coalesced in Moses, and this combination is needed, perhaps more than anything else today.

The Ten Commandments were introduced with signs and wonders. The date: approximately 1300 B.C. The place: the Sinai desert, which had become Moses' new home. It was there that the Lord said to Moses, "I am going to come to you in a dense cloud, so that people will hear me speaking with you and will always put their trust in you" (Exod. 19:9).

Something big was obviously afoot, for the Lord said to Moses:

> Go to the people and consecrate them today and tomorrow. Have them wash their clothes and be ready by the third day, because on that day the LORD will come down on Mount Sinai in the sight of all the people. Put limits for the people around the mountain and tell them, "Be careful that you do not go up the mountain or touch the foot of it. Whoever touches the mountain shall surely be put to death."
>
> —EXODUS 19:10–12

There followed thunder and lightning, with a thick cloud over the mountain, and a very loud trumpet blast. Everyone in the camp trembled. Mount Sinai was covered with smoke, "because the LORD descended on it in fire. The smoke billowed up from it like smoke from a furnace; the whole mountain trembled violently, and the sound of the trumpet grew louder and louder" (Exod. 19:18–19). The sight and sound were so terrifying that Moses later said that he trembled with fear (Heb. 12:21). For God was angry with Israel. Moses later said to them, "I feared the anger and wrath of the LORD, for he was angry enough with you to destroy you" (Deut. 9:19).

The apostle Paul was to pick up on this when he explained the reason God gave the Law in the first place:

What, then, was the purpose of the Law? It was added because of transgressions until the Seed to whom the promise referred had come.

—GALATIANS 3:19

THE PURPOSE OF THE LAW

So why do we have the Ten Commandments? We have the Ten Commandments today, strangely enough, because of Israel's transgressions. We are the beneficiaries of Israel's wickedness. In other words, we have the benefit of the Ten Commandments because Israel needed to be restrained. Arguably, had Israel not sinned there never would have been the Ten Commandments. We are thankful for them, so there is an ironic sense of gratitude for Israel's sinfulness. Because of the sin of ancient Israel, then, God stepped in to protect them from themselves. Without this restraint they would have destroyed themselves.

The Ten Commandments, then, were God's idea. They came directly from Him and not man. Could any human being ever have thought of the Ten Commandments? Only God could have come up with such an understanding of righteousness, laws so complete that in three thousand years they have never been improved upon. Like them or not, He knew what we needed. "For he knows how we are formed, he remembers that we are dust" (Ps. 103:14). God's Law is "perfect" (Ps. 19:7).

To put it another way, suppose one adopts the theology of the German philosopher Ludwig Feuerbach. He said that God is nothing more than man's projection upon the backdrop of the universe.[1] What did he mean by that? The idea is that God is created by man, that is, in man's mind; that man—frail and finite—wants to believe that there is a God out there who will take care of us and that when we die we can go to heaven. This is a crutch that gets us through life. God is just man's projection upon the backdrop of the universe.

Given that kind of reasoning, I ask, could man have projected the Ten Commandments? The answer is no. Man could not have come up with this. Because by nature man hates God, we hate righteousness. The Law was given because God's redeemed

54

people, the ancient children of Israel, were becoming rebellious and ungrateful. And so nobody has improved on them in three thousand years. They are complete and as perfect as you get. Man is not capable of coming up with these commandments.

However, we are not saved by the Ten Commandments. Why? Not because there is anything wrong with them, but because something is wrong with us (Rom. 8:3). And the interesting thing that we must never forget is that the Ten Commandments, though perfect and complete as far as you can go in having a moral code, are inferior to what Jesus taught in the Sermon on the Mount and what the Holy Spirit can lead one to be and to do. Jesus gave one application after another showing how the Holy Spirit leads a person to outclass the Law. There are things He did not elaborate on—which are found elsewhere in the New Testament—that show a love for God not commanded in the Law.

> The Ten Commandments cannot produce an inward righteousness; only an outward righteousness. An inward righteousness comes from the heart; an outward righteousness—to be seen—is what you do grudgingly, and that out of the fear of punishment.

For example, take the matter of rejoicing in the Lord. There is nothing in the Ten Commandments that would lead you to that—not even a hint of it, because there is nothing in them that would make you want to do it. They are inferior compared to the righteousness of the Holy Spirit. This is because the Ten Commandments cannot produce an inward righteousness; only an outward righteousness. An inward righteousness comes from the heart; an outward righteousness—to be seen—is what you do grudgingly, and that out of the fear of punishment. When the Law was given the motivation for keeping it was out of fear of punishment.

We are all like that to this day. Why do you stop when there is a red light? It is because you are afraid that perhaps some policeman will be around to see you if you go on through the red light. Presumably when traffic is busy you wouldn't do it, but sometimes late at night you think, "Why bother to stop here?" But why do you stop? You are afraid that maybe there will be that hidden camera out there that will flash and you will get caught.

I never will forget parking in a place in central London where I saw these white lines in the form of a big *X*, and I said to somebody, "What are these lines here for?"

"Oh, that's for a diplomat."

I said, "You know, that's not legal, that's not right. Who do they think they are, that they can park here?" I had to be someplace, and I thought, *I don't think this is right*. So I parked there. Well, after a couple of hours I came back, and there were the same zigzag lines but I did not see my car! And I had this sinking feeling, "Oh, no!" My worst fears were confirmed. They had taken my car, and I had to go several miles away by taxi to get it. Then there was a £35 fine, plus a £65 fee I had to pay to get my car back—plus the cost of the taxi. I can safely tell you, I no longer park where I see those lines!

The fear of punishment works. And that is how the ancient Law was enforced; it was an outward righteousness carried out grudgingly, but not because in their hearts the people particularly delighted in it.

At a place on the map, at a time in history, then, the Law came. In the Sinai desert around 1300 B.C., it came directly from God. Literally every word was from God—this is why they are unimprovable. The Law is inferior to what Jesus Himself taught because the Law is weak through the flesh. That means that you and I are powerless to keep it. There is nothing wrong with the Law, but there is a lot wrong with us. We are weak, sinful, frail human beings. This is why no man or woman ever kept the Law. This is why we needed a Redeemer to be followed by the coming of the Holy Spirit. Said Paul:

> For what the Law was powerless to do in that it was weakened by the sinful nature, God did by sending his own Son in the likeness of sinful man to be a sin offering. And so he condemned sin in sinful man, in order that the righteous requirements of the Law might be fully met in us, who do not live according to the sinful nature but according to the Spirit.
>
> —ROMANS 8:3–4

If the Law could save us, the Ten Commandments would do it. You are not going to improve upon them. But they cannot save us. Why then write about something that cannot save us? Why investigate the Ten Commandments? Let me give three reasons.

1. It is an essential part of God's Word. "All Scripture is God-breathed and is useful for teaching, rebuking, correcting and training in righteousness" (2 Tim. 3:16). "For prophecy never had its origin in the will of man, but men spoke from God as they were carried along by the Holy Spirit" (2 Pet. 1:21). Any part of God's Word is worthy of careful examination.

2. It was the standard, and remains the standard, of the righteousness God wants for His people. He wants it to this day, yet the Christian goes beyond it by walking in the Spirit. This is what Jesus meant by the righteousness that surpasses that of the scribes and Pharisees (Matt. 5:20).

3. Since the New Testament refers many times to the Law, we should know what that means. We should also see why it is—as I shall show—that the law of Christ, the law of love, or walking in the Spirit is a higher standard than that set by the Ten Commandments.

This leads to the big question, to what extent are the Ten Commandments relevant today? Do you have to keep the Ten Commandments to be a Christian? If not, what is their relevance for the Christian? I will answer that question. In this chapter I want to show the purpose of the Law, the reason for the Ten Commandments. I will try to explain Paul's answer when he asks, "What was the purpose of the Law?"

We need to know first of all why he asks the question. Have you ever asked that question? The reason Paul asks the question is because he had just demonstrated why we are not saved by the Law. In a word: it is because our model in the Old Testament is not Moses or the Law, but Abraham. Abraham lived 430 years before the coming of the Law (Gal. 3:17). He lived very well without the Law. He believed the gospel (Gal. 3:8) and lived a godly life by walking in the Spirit. All this, I repeat, without the Law, for it came more than four hundred years later. The fact that the Law later came did not set aside what God had done through Abraham, including the covenant God made with Abraham and his seed. This is because we are all a part of the seed of Abraham by faith. And for this reason Paul began saying we are not under the Law. Why? We go back to Abraham.

It will be recalled that the Law is a parenthesis in God's salvation history. The Law came in as an extra; it was "added" (Rom. 5:20; Gal. 3:19). Once we trust what Jesus did for us on the cross—when the Law was fulfilled—we are in effect put back into Abraham's position who believed the gospel and was saved before there was such a thing as God's Law. We are therefore not "under" the Law. "Now that faith has come, we are no longer under the supervision of the law" (Gal. 3:25). This does not mean we are given liberty to live in an ungodly manner—quite the contrary. We are led by the Spirit, who leads to holy living (Gal. 5:16).

Paul therefore had to deal with the question, what was the purpose of the Law? He answers: "It was added because of transgressions until the Seed [meaning Christ] to whom the promise referred had come" (Gal. 3:19).

This Law, including the Ten Commandments, was imposed on a redeemed community, the ancient people of Israel. The word *redeemed* means "bought back." Israel had sinned, and the people were on the verge of losing their way entirely. In Exodus 6:6 God said, "I will free you from being slaves…and will redeem you with an outstretched arm and with mighty acts of judgment." This began with the Passover when God struck down all the firstborn in Egypt. What saved Israel was their putting the blood of a lamb over the top and on both sides of their doors. God promised, "When I see the blood, I will pass over you" (Exod. 12:13). After that came the whole people of Israel crossing the Red Sea on dry land. Then Moses sang, "In your unfailing love you will lead the people you have redeemed" (Exod. 15:13). In a word, then, they were now bought back; God owned them. God bought them back through the shedding of blood.

Passover was the beginning of what could now be called the sacrificial system. This was part of the ceremonial Law, how God was to be worshiped. Shortly after the giving of the Law, God made an agreement with the people. This agreement became known as the covenant. A covenant is an agreement between two parties that is based upon certain conditions. Moses read "the Book of the Covenant...to the people. They responded, 'We will do everything the LORD has said; we will obey'" (Exod. 24:7). It was at that point that the plan of shed blood became a part of the covenant because, "Moses then took the blood, sprinkled it on the people and said, 'This is the blood of the covenant that the LORD has made with you in accordance with all these words'" (v. 8).

However, the writer of Hebrews concludes, "It is impossible for the blood of bulls and goats to take away sins" (Heb. 10:4). Jesus was the fulfillment of the old sacrificial system. On the cross he offered "for all time one sacrifice for sins" (Heb. 10:12). As Peter put it, "For you know that it was not with perishable things such as silver or gold that you were redeemed from the empty way of life handed down to you from your forefathers, but with the precious blood of Christ, a lamb without blemish or defect" (1 Pet. 1:18–19).

The word *redeemed* is a word that Paul used in Galatians 3:14: God "redeemed us in order that the blessing given to Abraham might come to the Gentiles through Christ Jesus." He had just said in verse 13: "He redeemed us from the curse of the law." That means we have been bought back. For as I said, that is what the word *redeemed* means, and it is a word the New Testament uses to show how we are saved. In other words, we have been bought— purchased, paid for—by the blood of Jesus.

Whoever you are, you have been bought and paid for— redeemed by the blood of Jesus. You may say, "Well, not me." Yes, you. Because when Jesus died, He died for everybody (2 Cor. 5:14– 15). He bought you with His blood, which means you are not your own (1 Cor. 6:19–20). You may be living as though it is "your" life and you say, "Don't tell me I am not my own." I must tell you that you are bought with a price. The reason you can't get away with doing things without feeling awful inside is because of the way God made you. As St. Augustine put it, "Thou hast made us for thyself, our hearts are restless until they find their repose in thee." Or as Blaise Pascal put it, "There is a God-shaped blank in every man." You can say, "I am going to do it my way," but you will end up being so sorry; it does not work well on your own. For you are bought with a price.

Israel was bought with a price, and her redemption began to unfold at what is called "Passover." That is a Jewish word; it is a biblical word. What does it mean? Israel was under the bondage of Pharaoh in Egypt. One day God told Israel to take the blood of a lamb and sprinkle the blood on both doorposts and on the lintel over the top of the door. In Cecil B. DeMille's *The Ten Commandments* there was only a fleeting, passing glimpse of that awesome sight. I wish more attention had been given to it. There were certain places in Egypt, had you gone there that night, you would have seen blood of lambs spattered on both sides of the door and over the top. And God said, "I am going to come through Egypt that night and kill every firstborn male, including animals. But when I come to a house where I see blood, I will pass over it—I will pass over you." (See Exodus 12:12–13.) And so that was the night that the blood, later fulfilled by the blood of Jesus Christ, saved the people of Israel.

Fifty days later, after they had been delivered from Pharaoh and crossed the Red Sea on dry land, God gave the Law—the Ten Commandments. Fifty days after Passover also became known as Pentecost. And so, nearly two thousand years ago, fifty days after Jesus died on the cross the Holy Spirit came down on the people who had been waiting (Acts 2:1–4). It could easily be forgotten that Pentecost was the commemoration of God giving the Law at Sinai. This is extremely significant. For the Holy Spirit replaced the Law as our immediate guide into all truth (John 16:13). So Paul said, "But if you are led by the Spirit, you are not under law" (Gal. 5:18). The Holy Spirit given at Pentecost was the fulfillment of all that God intended by the Law. The Law was God's way of enforcing gratitude. Not that the people were grateful. God was forcing His ancient people to respond to His redeeming them by fear of punishment. Their keeping the Law was what they promised to do, yes, but they were also forced to do it. But when the Spirit came down it was what they wanted to do; it came from inside.

And that is the way the Spirit operates in us to this day.

So Israel's redemption began to unfold at Passover. God did not save Israel because they were Law-abiding! God saved them from Egypt without any Law at all. Sinai did not lead to Passover, but Passover to Sinai. Let me explain what that means. It is because they had been redeemed that the Law was given. We are not given the Law in order to get to Passover. We are not given the Law in order that we might be redeemed and then be assured that God has accepted us. That is the very reason some people have never been assured that they are really Christians. They thought that before they could be saved they had to keep the Law; they had to keep the Ten Commandments first. And if they have kept them they can, hopefully, start trusting the promise. Wrong. Do you know, the moment you start at Sinai and try to work your way to Passover you will always be trusting yourself. Every time.

My wife, Louise, and I went to Pensacola in the summer of 1997. I do believe that God began doing a great work there at Brownsville Assembly of God. But my heart sank as I began to hear what I feel was a legalistic type of preaching that was reminiscent of what I had come across in the British Museum under the reading of these Puritans; it was just like what I was taught before I had my "Damascus road experience." And I thought it was so sad that there in Pensacola where God was at work they were imposing a legalism on people, because the impression given was that if you stop doing this and you stop doing that, then you come to the mercy seat.

That is not the way we are saved. We need to know that God sent His Son who died on a cross, who by Himself kept the Law, and we are saved not by keeping the Law but by trusting what Jesus did for us on the cross. Sinai did not lead to Passover, but Passover led to Sinai. If we trust what Jesus did for us on the cross, then the Spirit will lead us to godly living that will actually exceed the righteousness of the Law.

Here is what happened. God wanted Israel to express gratitude for what He had done for them. But they were beginning to be ungrateful. And so He imposed commands that needed to be obeyed—I call it enforced gratitude, as if (as I said) God put a pistol to their heads to obey. And the Law was imposed on Israel because Israel needed a restraint on their wickedness. This is why

Paul says, "What is the purpose of the Law?" Answer: "It was added because of transgressions" (Gal. 3:19).

So Israel had begun to show ingratitude for what God had done for them, and this unthankfulness emerged in a very short period of time. It is so sad to think that after God had delivered them from Pharaoh in just a few days they began to complain and to tiptoe into idolatry. So God said, "Stop it!" and brought in the Law. Then the Law became binding on Israel in a number of ways.

For example, health and prosperity were irrevocably tied to their obedience to the Law. The "health and wealth gospel" would be categorically true if Christians were under the Law. They were obliged to keep the whole, not just a part, of the Law; they couldn't be selective. They couldn't go through the Ten Commandments and say, "Well, I will try that one." No. You had to accept the whole package. In a word, the Law restrained sin by fear of punishment and promoted obedience by promise of reward. This is unfolded in Deuteronomy 27:26, which says: "Cursed is the man who does not uphold the words of this law by carrying them out."

Then God promised blessings for obedience.

> If you fully obey the LORD your God and carefully follow all his commands that I give you today, the LORD your God will set you high above all the nations on earth. All these blessings will come upon you and accompany you if you obey the LORD your God.
> —DEUTERONOMY 28:1–2

THE LAW AND GRACE

But what Paul tells us in Galatians 3:19 is that the Law was, as I said in chapter one, a parenthesis. Now a parenthesis is something added to a sentence and then put in brackets. So the Law was added; it was an addition. Romans 5:20 says the same thing; it was "added." It is a translation of a Greek word that literally means it came in aside; it is just parenthetical. So, as a sentence could be read by omitting what is in the brackets, so the plan of salvation is to be understood without the parenthesis of the Law. If you can, think for a moment chronologically: in about 1700 B.C. Abraham was justified by believing the promise, made righteous because he believed what God told him. And God said, "You are saved." Four hundred thirty years later the Law came in, but Paul says that Law was a parenthesis—added—a parenthesis only between Abraham and Jesus. And when Jesus came, He fulfilled the Law, which meant that what was promised to Abraham—who saw Christ's day and was "glad" (John 8:56)—was fulfilled in Christ. Therefore by believing the promise we are saved, like Abraham was. The Law has no bearing on whether we are saved.

The gospel was virtually complete in itself in Abraham before the Law came in. The plan of salvation is given as though there never had been the Law in the first place. We are saved by faith alone, and so Paul says in Galatians 3:6, "Consider Abraham: 'He believed God, and it was credited to him as righteousness.'" And this is the way you and I are saved. We are not saved because we are now going to start keeping the Law. We are not saved because from today we are going to stop doing this, and we are going to start doing that, and then somehow say, "Now I can trust the blood of Jesus." If that continues to be our way of trying to be saved we will never be saved. We must begin with the fact that Jesus in Himself perfectly performed all that God required, so when we are saved, it is because Jesus paid our debt and we put all of our trust in Him. So we are saved by faith alone. And when Abraham was saved, there was no Law! Never forget that Abraham achieved a high level of godliness without the Law.

The Law, then, came in 430 years after Abraham. That is why we call the Law a parenthesis, meaning the time between Abraham and Christ. As Christians, we take our cue from Abraham. For Jesus said, "[Abraham] saw [my day] and was glad" (John 8:56).

Now some will want to say at this point, that means the Ten Commandments have no relevance for the Christian. Wrong. I am not finished yet. Remember this: Abraham by the Spirit fulfilled what the Law would later bring in. Let me explain. He was justified by faith; he walked in the Spirit. He was not under the Law, but he nonetheless fulfilled what the Law would come to be by his godly life. So if you had shown Abraham the Ten Commandments, despite his imperfections, he would have said, "Well, that is the way I have chosen to live."

The relevance of the Ten Commandments for the Christian is that they serve as a backdrop by which we can partly see if we are walking in the Spirit. Because if we were to walk in the Spirit, we would fulfill the Law "accidentally," even if we had never heard of the Ten Commandments! And yet, looking at the whole of the Law, no human being ever kept it perfectly. Because if you were able to keep the whole of the Ten Commandments you would never sin. But it was never assumed that anybody would keep the Ten Commandments perfectly.

Now you could possibly keep the first nine outwardly. It is possible not to commit adultery. It is possible not to murder. It is possible not to misuse God's name. It is possible not to lie about your neighbor. But once you get to the tenth commandment, "You shall not covet" and you truly see the implications of that, you begin to see that you hadn't really kept the first nine after all. And this is the point Jesus made when He explained the Law in the Sermon on the Mount (Matt. 5:21–48).

So Jesus made a daring statement when He said, "Do not think that I have come to abolish the Law or the Prophets; I have not come to abolish them but to fulfill them" (Matt. 5:17). Jesus performed the Ten Commandments perfectly. He's the first person ever to do it. That is the reason we need His perfect life, as well as His death as our substitute on the cross (Rom. 5:10). He was our substitute. The life He lived for thirty-three years is that to which we point as being our righteousness (1 Cor. 1:30). The whole of the life of Jesus was for you and for me. He did not die for Himself. He did not keep the Law for Himself. He was doing it for you and me. Therefore the way I am converted is to put all my trust in a substitute, in another person who kept that Law for me—every day of His life in thought and word and deed. Therefore when I trust what He did for me on the cross I recognize that by His sinless life He became a substitute: His blood paid my debt and bought me. So He performed the Ten Commandments perfectly.

In a word, Christ fulfilled the Law. We fulfill it, therefore, because our faith counts for righteousness as though we kept it. We walk in the Spirit. That does not mean we are sinless. Let me tell you why we will never be without sin in this life. Only Jesus had the Holy Spirit without measure. "For the one whom God has sent speaks the words of God, for God gives the Spirit without limit" (John 3:34). That means Jesus had all the Holy Spirit there is. We have a little bit of the Spirit, if I may put it that way; only Jesus had the Spirit without measure. He lived perfectly, He had a perfect faith, and He was in perfect obedience to the Law. Our faith, then, is in measure (Rom. 12:3). We are going to slip; we are going to fall. We will not be perfect and be like Him until we are in heaven. We only have a measure of faith; that is, we have a limit to our faith.

What then is the place of the Law for us? Since Christ kept it for us, what place has it for us? The apostle Paul said, "We know that the Law is good if one uses it properly" (1 Tim. 1:8). What is the proper use of the Law?

1. It shows the righteousness that God requires.
2. It shows the righteousness that Christ fulfilled as our substitute.
3. It serves as a backdrop by which we can tell if we are walking in the Spirit.

Obedience to the Spirit will express gratitude for what God has done for us, not because God has put a pistol to our heads, but because we want to honor Him and please Him. But even when we are fulfilling the Law by the Spirit it is good to have the Ten Commandments to consult.

My beloved friend Dr. William Greathouse used to tell this story. It seems that there was this very unhappily married couple who had continual tension in their marriage because the wife did not come up to her husband's standards. He had a list of rules for her to keep. He got angry when she failed, even though, under duress, she tried so hard. It was an unhappy marriage, but the husband died.

The lady later remarried. It was a happy marriage. She never dreamed she could be so happy. She felt loved, and there was no list of rules. One day, cleaning out a chest of drawers, she came across her former husband's list of rules. She sat down and read them. To her amazement, she found that she was keeping those old rules in the new marriage without even trying!

Said Paul:

For example, by law a married woman is bound to her husband as long as he is alive, but if her husband dies, she is released from the law of marriage....So, my brothers, you also died to the law through the body of Christ, that you might belong to another, to him who was raised from the dead, in order that we might bear fruit to God....But now, by dying to what once bound us, we have been released from the law so that we serve in the new way of the Spirit, and not in the old way of the written code.

—ROMANS 7:2–6

The Law also gives wisdom for a godless society. Paul went on to say:

We also know that law is made not for the righteous but for lawbreakers and rebels, the ungodly and sinful, the unholy and irreligious; for those who kill their fathers or mothers, for murderers, for adulterers and perverts, for slave traders and liars and perjurers—and for whatever else is contrary to the sound doctrine that conforms to the glorious gospel of the blessed God, which he entrusted to me.

—1 TIMOTHY 1:9–11

The Law gives great wisdom for a society so that it will reflect order and so that the people in it protect one another. This is why Proverbs 14:34 says, "Righteousness exalts a nation, but sin is a disgrace to any people."

There is however a paradox in the Law. The word *paradox* means something that seems contradictory. There are, in fact, two paradoxes.

The first is, we keep it, and yet we do not. We walk in the Spirit; we keep it—we live in love; we will keep it. Because Romans 13 points out that if we walk in love then we will fulfill the Law (v. 10). The problem is, nobody walks perfectly in the Spirit. And no one walks perfectly in love. This is why John said, "If we claim to be without sin, we deceive ourselves and the truth is not in us" (1 John 1:8).

The second paradox is, though the Law neither justifies

nor sanctifies, it is not wrong to consult it, because it is God's hint at how we should live our lives. So it is, I say, a backdrop to test whether we have been walking in the Spirit. Let me further explain what I mean by that. Suppose you say to me that you are walking in the Spirit—but you are committing adultery. Well, I would have to say that you are not walking in the Spirit. You say, "I am walking in the Spirit," but you are not honoring your parents? You are not walking in the Spirit. You say, "I am walking in the Spirit," but you are lying about your neighbor? You are not walking in the Spirit. And so you could go through the whole of the Ten Commandments. They all show us a backdrop as a test of whether or not we are walking in the Spirit, after all.

The Law will never serve as a reliable basis by which you can know you are saved. If you look to the Law to know whether you are saved, there will always be a doubt. I can tell you how to know that you are saved. When you believe that Jesus kept the Law for you and you are putting your trust in a substitute who shed His blood and bought you, who owns you, and you say, "I am going to trust what He did, and I know I am saved because He died for me"—that way the Law, if you fail to keep it, cannot touch you—then you are secure in what Jesus did for you.

That, then, is how you know you are saved. One of my favorite hymns puts it like this:

> I need no other argument,
> I need no other plea;
> It is enough that Jesus died,
> And that He died for me.[2]

During those days when I was working on my thesis and began to think, "Is this why I am here?", I almost lost a sense of the gospel. It was all legalism, all what I do, and I thought, *This is not what God showed me.* And I am so thankful that He brought me through, and I can tell you now—that I've got one hope of getting to heaven. It is not because I keep the Law, I can tell you that. I have one hope.

It is enough that Jesus died, and that He died for me.

Chapter 6

THE FIRST COMMANDMENT: THE TRUE GOD

You shall have no other gods before me.

—EXODUS 20:3

THE TEN COMMANDMENTS are God's teaching, God teaching His people—those who were special to Him— about Himself. The Ten Commandments represent the minimum standard of righteousness God wants and demands of His people. It is a standard that would never be lowered. For in the New Testament, with the coming of the Holy Spirit, the standard is even higher than that of the Ten Commandments. Paul calls it "Christ's law" (1 Cor. 9:21). It means totally forgiving those who have hurt us, refusing to judge those who have been unjust. It is bearing one another's burdens, for doing this fulfills the "law of Christ" (Gal. 6:2). No Pharisee imagined such a lifestyle. This is why it surpasses the righteousness of the Pharisees. The first commandment, "You shall have no other gods before me," is designed to show us basically what God is like as well as what is best and right for us.

The Ten Commandments are in a logical order. There are those who, when they teach the commandments, start at the tenth and work backward. There is something to be said for that. After all, the tenth commandment, "You shall not covet," really opens up all of them, as does our approach in this book by beginning with the Sermon on the Mount. It was the tenth commandment, as we will see later, which made the apostle Paul see his own sin (Rom. 7:7). So there is nothing wrong with starting with the tenth and working backward. But having begun with the Sermon on the Mount, I have chosen to work through the Ten Commandments in their original order. For what we have in the first command is the foundation for all the rest.

The first three commands deal with God and what God is like. The first commandment is designed to show God's unique reality but also to show how He will not allow anything in our lives that competes with Him. "You shall have no other gods"—small g—"before me." What would another god be? It would be an idol. It would be something that would compete with the true God. The second command shows His way of being worshiped. The third command shows His honor and glory—the glory of His name. In looking at these first three commandments I raise the question, is God insecure?

The word *insecure* means a feeling of being unsafe, being vulnerable, or being threatened. Is God threatened? Is He threatened by other gods? Is He afraid that you will discover one of these gods and find that they are better than Himself and so He wants to keep you from the knowledge of these other gods? Sometimes those who appear to be very powerful are actually very insecure. A dictator of a country, whether right-wing or left-wing, is very insecure. Did you know that a monarch may be very insecure? I shall soon answer the question about God's insecurity, but first a word about gratitude.

GRATITUDE

What we have in the Ten Commandments is not only enforced learning but enforced gratitude. God is showing His people how He demands gratitude. The difference, however, between being under the Law and being Christians not under the Law is this: under the Law it was enforced, "You shall have no other gods before me."

But as Christians our walk in the Spirit is spontaneous. We do not want any other gods. So what we have in the Ten Commandments is God's way of teaching gratitude.

Gratitude is a way of summarizing the Christian doctrine of sanctification. The doctrine of sanctification could be called the doctrine of gratitude. Sanctification refers to the process of becoming holy, or the process by which you are made holy. This process begins when you are converted and is consummated when you are glorified. This means that when you get to heaven you will be perfectly holy and there will be no way of improvement. But in the meantime, here below, it is a process. Once you become a Christian you begin a life of holiness. In the Old Testament it was enforced; in the New Testament it comes because you love God.

The reason sanctification is the doctrine of gratitude is because it has nothing to do with whether you get to heaven. Nothing. Gratitude is that which shows we are thankful, and God puts us on our honor to show gratitude. Let me put it another way. I love it when, having heard the gospel, somebody asks the question, "Well, why bother to be godly, or why bother to live the Christian life, or why bother to show good works?" I love this question because I know they've understood what I just said to them! If they do not ask such a question, the chances are that they have not grasped the gospel.

It is at this point, if you have really understood the message, that you may well say, "Oh, well, why bother to live a life of good works and doing good?" And now I come up with the answer: we live a life of gratitude to God. It is by walking in the Holy Spirit; because once you become a Christian you are given the Holy Spirit and that Holy Spirit will lead you to a holy life.

The Ten Commandments were enforced gratitude. The Holy Spirit is an enabling gratitude. And yet we need to be taught to be grateful. If I've sought to do anything over the years, I've sought to teach people to be thankful. Because I know this about God: He likes to be thanked. He loves gratitude. He loves praise. He loves worship.

A JEALOUS GOD

Now I want to answer the question, "Is God afraid that we might prefer another god to Him?" The answer is, yes. Not because He is insecure, but because He knows what we are like. Because of man's nature. We were born with a sinful nature, and I will try to explain.

The first man and the first woman, Adam and Eve in the Garden of Eden (which was a place on the map and a date in history), were created without sin. It is hard for us to imagine what this is like, for this is not the way you and I were born. David put it like this, "Surely I was sinful at birth, sinful from the time my mother conceived me" (Ps. 51:5). We are no different, and we come from our mother's womb speaking lies (Ps. 58:3). St. Augustine described four stages of all people:

1. Created able to sin (that was Adam and Eve before the Fall)
2. Not able not to sin (that was Adam and Eve after the Fall)
3. Able not to sin (that is the potential of a person who has been redeemed)
4. Not able to sin (that is the way we will be in heaven)

Not one of us was born as Adam was before the Fall. We have inherited the condition he caused by his sin. We call this sin the Fall, a historic moment that determined the condition of all people who were to be born thereafter. We may wish that Adam and Eve had not sinned. But they sinned, and the moment they sinned something happened. Death set in. They lived on for a number of years, but eventually they died; they wouldn't have died had they not sinned.

If you never sinned, you'd never die. But what happened was, all of those born thereafter were born as Adam and Eve became, not as they were when they were first created. If we were born as Adam and Eve were made before they sinned, then the theoretical possibility exists that some human being out there would never sin. But we all sin. There never has been a perfect person. The reason is that we are born sinners. We are already sinners, and that is why we sin. There is, therefore, the proneness to evil. This is why a baby does not need to be taught to lie. This is why a baby does not need to be taught to be selfish or to lose its little temper. We are born that way.

Because of our nature we are tempted by anything other than the true God, and that is why God has brought these commands to us: because we need them. It is not because He is insecure but because He knows what man is like. Furthermore, when God said, "You shall have no other gods before me," Israel was already in the presence of God. That is the assumption, because this is a word to God's special people. So He says, "You shall have no other gods before me." The Hebrew means "in my presence." So Israel was in the presence of God. God would not tolerate another god in His presence. God will not tolerate any idol among His special people. The people of Israel were a chosen people, and they were being prepared for a special land.

The first commandment is written to make us aware that we are doing everything before God. All that we do is before Him. He sees everything that is going on. All things are open and naked before His eyes (Heb. 4:13). Nothing misses Him. He is perfectly observant. Nothing escapes God's notice. So if there is anything in your life that, the moment you begin to indulge in it, causes your love for God and holiness to diminish—holy things, purity, and righteousness—God says, "It is not OK. Stop it! You will have no other gods before me." This first command refers to three things:

1. *God is unique.* Why would it refer to the uniqueness of God? Because the true God, the God of the Bible, is the only God who has no beginning. The first question a child will ask when he begins to be aware of teaching about God is, "Daddy, Mommy, who made God?" Or, "Where did God come from?" And the answer is, nobody made God; God has always been. How do we grasp this? We are not capable of grasping this. But because He is from everlasting to everlasting He's the only true God. All other gods have a beginning. They were created—by man.

2. *All that exists was created by God.* "'To whom will you compare me? Or who is my equal?' says the Holy One. Lift your eyes and look to the heavens: Who created all these? He who brings out the starry host one by one, and calls them each by name. Because of his great power and mighty strength, not one of them is missing" (Isa. 40:25–26). "You are worthy, our Lord and God, to receive glory and honor and power, for you created all things, and by your will they were created and have their being" (Rev. 4:11).

3. *God alone is the living God.* He is alive. Psalm 115:3–4 says, "Our God is in heaven; he does whatever pleases him. But their idols are silver and gold, made by the hands of men." And so any idol is made by man's hands. The biblical writers love to refer to the fact that the true God is living. "See to it, brothers, that none of you has a sinful, unbelieving heart that turns away from the living God" (Heb. 3:12). Our hope is in "the living God" (1 Tim. 4:10). We are a part of "the church of the living God" (1 Tim. 3:15). We have turned from idols to serve "the living and true God" (1 Thess. 1:9). "It is a dreadful thing to fall into the hands of the living God" (Heb. 10:31).

What is your idol? Is it money? Your job? A human being? Television? Are you watching things on television that you know in your heart grieve the Holy Spirit? The proof of a high level of spirituality—the proof that the Holy Spirit is in you ungrieved, is that you are likely to feel Him being grieved the very moment you do something you shouldn't do. One bit of evidence that you are not very spiritual is that it takes you a long time to realize that you have grieved God. I sometimes define spirituality as closing the time gap between sin and repentance. For example, how long does it take you to admit that you have sinned? How long does it take you to admit you were wrong? How long does it take you to admit that you have grieved the Holy Spirit? For some it takes months. For some it takes a few weeks. For some it takes a few days. For some it takes a few hours. For some it takes a few minutes. For some it takes a few seconds. And if you can narrow the time gap to seconds, you are getting there.

For when you are truly Spirit-filled and truly enjoying the ungrieved Spirit, you will be likely to sense it immediately when you grieve Him. When you say a word that you shouldn't say, when you look at something you shouldn't look at, when you listen to something and think, *I shouldn't be hearing this*, and immediately inside you feel awful, it shows a highly developed sensitivity to the Holy Spirit. On the other hand, when I feel nothing at all if I hold a grudge, lose my temper, listen to unkind gossip, or indulge in anything that is not honoring to God, it is a dead giveaway that I am not where I ought to be with God.

I will tell you also what is likely to happen if you do not follow an impulse of the Spirit. The next time, you will not feel anything. A lady asked Arthur Blessitt why God seems to speak so clearly to him but not to her. He replied, "Did you ever feel an impulse to talk to someone you did not know about the Lord?"

"Yes," she replied.

"Start obeying that impulse," replied Arthur, "and that voice will get clearer and clearer."

But when we do not obey that impulse we will wake up one day and realize that we never get such a prompting any more. And that is why you can go like this for days or weeks or months. One hopes mercifully something will happen that will make you realize that God is grieved—that He does not like any disobedience at all. The only thing to do is to come to Him in repentance and say, "I am sorry." You will not grow in grace until you do it. That will show that you really do not want to grieve God; it will show that you do not want to have any other gods before Him.

> When you are truly Spirit-filled and truly enjoying the ungrieved Spirit, you will be likely to sense it immediately when you grieve Him.

The uniqueness of God. He had no beginning; all that exists was created by God. He alone is the living God. The idols have mouths, but they cannot speak; eyes, but they cannot see; ears, but they cannot hear; noses, but they cannot smell; hands, but they cannot feel; feet, but they cannot walk, nor can they utter a sound from their throats. And yet, do you know, people will want those gods! Why? It is not even rational.

The reason God says, "You shall have no other gods before me," is because our hearts are so corrupt and we are so wicked that we will actually take on board something like that. When I read through the Books of Samuel, Kings, and Chronicles, I continue to be amazed over how Israel would settle for a king who would take them right back to the worship of Baal. I think, *Why don't they learn? Why would anybody want to do that?* It is because our hearts are anti-God by nature. And God knows that.

The uniqueness of God. And yet, He alone has the capacity to love and to care, and that is why He gave this command—not because He's insecure but because He does not want you to wreck your life. He does not want you to grieve His Holy Spirit. He does not want you to have to live with the guilt and the pain of letting another god come in and divert you. I sometimes think that the most painful feeling in the world—bar none—is guilt. The feeling that you are to blame and have to live with certain consequences is a heaviness of spirit for which there is no sure cure other than the grace of God. It is God in His graciousness who gives the first command in order to spare us this guilt.

The God of the Bible is the only God who has a Son, an eternal Son Jesus Christ. He was God as though He were not man, and man as though He were not God. And yet when He says, "You shall have no other gods before me," He uses what I can only call accommodating language by referring to them as gods. After all, in Isaiah 45:21 He says, "There is no God apart from me." And yet in the first commandment He calls them gods because idols can have a grip on you.

The first commandment refers to the self-understanding of God, God's understanding of Himself. He knows Himself. The great philosopher Socrates' philosophy can be summed up in two words: "Know yourself." People today search to know themselves by reading philosophy, Buddha, and Confucius. They somehow think that an Asian religion has something beyond the Bible. Or they go into psychoanalysis and get a psychiatrist who will take them back to their childhood. They want to know themselves.

I talked to a psychiatrist who gives psychoanalysis. He actually said to me, "It does not help a person all that much at the end of the day." He said, "They come for two or three years, and they are not much closer to understanding and mastering themselves." And this was not a Christian!

The mind is insatiable, and we never get enough. You may be trying all kinds of things to get into yourself. The first commandment is the first positive step toward getting to know yourself. Why? Because it comes from a God who understands Himself. He makes no apology. He says, "I am the one; I know everything. I can do anything. I am everywhere."

It also means that we can understand Him—a little. Not fully, but a little bit. We will never understand God perfectly—in this life or in heaven. One thing that will make heaven heavenly is that we will be ever learning and able to grasp the truth. Sadly, in this life there are those, said Paul, who are "always learning but never able to acknowledge the truth" (2 Tim. 3:7). But by giving us this first commandment God kindly unveils something of His nature and whets our appetite for more of Him. And yet it is not a total understanding that we enjoy. But that little bit of understanding of the true God will also give you more understanding of yourself than you ever had in your life! You can read history, psychology, architecture, or art, and you will still want to know more, not learning what really matters. So think about it: in the last days people will be "always learning but never able to acknowledge the truth." Isn't that awful? And so there is a little bit of God we can begin to understand. You can take a major step this moment by receiving His Son as your Savior, and you can get more understanding the first week of your being a Christian than you had in your whole life. That is a promise.

Understanding God is what helps us toward understanding ourselves. We are all made in God's image (Gen. 1:27). It follows that, by knowing God, we know ourselves. To try to grasp what we are by means of bypassing the knowledge of our Creator is to see ourselves as animals. "Man is what he eats," said Feuerbach,[1] which means that there is nothing beyond our physical bodies. The whole man is body and soul (or spirit). We know God not by our brain alone but by the "spirit within" us (1 Cor. 2:11). Once our human spirit responds to God's Holy Spirit, we begin to tap into that dimension of ourselves that could otherwise never be explored. We also see the negative side, which we would otherwise want to dismiss. God knows that we are like sheep who go astray. I learned some things about sheep from Douglas Macmillan, a shepherd from Scotland who is now in heaven. He became a Christian and began preaching. He said, "A sheep will always think that the grass is greener on the other side of the fence." God says we are like sheep. It is by the Holy Spirit, moreover, that we admit this to ourselves. "We all, like sheep, have gone astray, each of us has turned to his own way" (Isa. 53:6).

God knows that we are all like that. He knows what man is like, the tendency to follow after other gods. The further we get from God, the more we begin to think that other religions are not so bad. Part of the way we can recognize if a person is backsliding is if he has begun to think sympathetically toward the idea that other religions have their validity, that if their practitioners are sincere they will get to heaven. If you are beginning to think like that, I must say that you are in danger of backsliding, or quite possibly you have never been saved.

The closer you get to God, the more you will see that He, the God of the Bible, sent His Son who said, "I am the way, the truth and the life. No one comes to the Father except through me" (John 14:6). So I do not care if pastors or prominent Christians say that there is more than one way, that it does not have to be just through Jesus Christ—they are either apostate, have never been converted, or are backsliders and in a bad spiritual state. But the closer you get to God and the more you walk in the Spirit, the more you will affirm His uniqueness and know that through His Son is the only way to be saved.

God also knows how the demonic gets in the moment we become attracted to anything that competes with the true God. The apostle Paul said this in 1 Corinthians 10:18–22 when he talked about those who offer sacrifices to idols and then eat of the meat that had been sacrificed to the idols. He said that once they eat that meat, they should remember that the sacrifices of pagans are offered to demons, not to God. He continued, "I do not want you to be participants with demons."

The moment you flirt around with anything that is counterfeit to the true God, the devil will perch upon your shoulder and look for any other opportunity to get in. For example, do not even read an astrology chart. Don't even, out of curiosity, say, "I wonder what it would be for me today." You may say, "I do not really believe in it," but you read it. Do that, and the devil will get a hook in some way. Don't ever play with a Ouija board. When you walk near a shop that offers anything occultic, I would even suggest that you ask the blood of Jesus to cover you; do not even go near the place. Don't play around with anything that is occultic or demonic. Don't wear a good luck charm. Why? The devil gets in, and you will become vulnerable to the counterfeit. God knows what is best for us.

This first commandment even refers to God's urgency. Why was this the first command? Because this is what is needed first. The first thing you should know in your gratitude toward God is that you are going to put Him first. The moment you ask the Holy Spirit to come into your life you are denouncing and rejecting any competition with God.

Finally, when God said, "You shall have no other gods before me"—it is very interesting—it is in the second person singular. "You"—He means you as an individual. That is surprising since this was given to all Israel. You would have thought it would be second person plural. But it is "you." That means He is talking to you. And to me.

Chapter 7

THE SECOND COMMANDMENT:
THE HIDDENNESS OF GOD

> You shall not make for yourself an idol in the
> form of anything in heaven above or on the earth
> beneath or in the waters below. You shall not
> bow down to them or worship them; for I, the
> LORD your God, am a jealous God, punishing
> the children for the sin of the fathers to the third
> and fourth generation of those who hate me, but
> showing love to a thousand generations of those
> who love me and keep my commandments.
>
> —EXODUS 20:4–6

DO YOU EVER wish God were different? You may say, "I do not believe in God at all." But let us assume that there is a God and that the true God is the God of the Bible, the God who reveals Himself in these words to the people of Israel. Are you happy about God being just like that? Or do you wish that He were different?

ACCEPTANCE

There are probably two kinds of people reading these lines. There are those who, if honest, would change God if they could. They would say, "Yes, I believe God is there, and I like this about Him, and I like that about Him, but I do not like everything." They would change God in some way if they could. But hopefully there are those in the second category who love God for being just as He is. They wouldn't change anything about Him.

As I get older, I find myself wanting to say to God, "Lord,

I love You for being just as You are." Why say this to Him? One reason is, because He likes it. He likes it because it affirms Him for being just as He is. Another reason—the main one: it is true.

Can you think of anything nicer than if someone were to say to you, "I like you just as you are"? That is rather nice, is it not? It is a wonderful feeling if someone gets to know you a little bit and says, "I like you just as you are." That is something that one's wife or husband would rather hear than anything, if you could say it and mean it!

We love to be accepted just as we are and to be loved just as we are.

Now I can tell you, in reverse, God loves you just as you are. He accepts you just as you are. And I do not know of anybody else like that—who accepts me just as I am and loves me just as I am. That is almost overwhelming, because I can think of so many things about me that I know are not good at all. God knows those things are there. After all, He made us. He is the one who chose our parents for us. And "he remembers that we are dust" (Ps. 103:14). If we can in turn say to Him, "Lord, I love You just as You are," it affirms Him. And so I say it to Him because I know He likes it. But I also say it to Him because it is true.

> It is difficult to understand God's ways or to feel His presence when bad things happen. But in those moments when I do not feel that touch and He hides His face, and I do not feel His presence, still I know that God's love never fails.

How could one say that when God has allowed things to happen to us, or to others, that are not pleasant? I know people who are suffering, and I am sure you do, too. Recent wars have caused difficult suffering to their victims. Hundreds of thousands of people in Africa and other places are starving. Every day in this nation mothers lose sons and daughters because of drunk drivers or cruel acts of murder.

It is difficult to understand God's ways or to feel His presence when bad things happen. But in those moments when I do not feel that touch and He hides His face, and I do not feel His presence, still I know that God's love never fails. We all have a story to tell.

But I love God for being just who He is. I love when His Holy Spirit is on me in great power, and I am filled with His goodness and am conscious of His presence. When His Spirit fills me to worship Him, I feel toward God as He feels toward Himself. I know that it is true. And in the same way, I also know that if I will wait a while, there will be an explanation for everything. Sometimes we get an explanation quickly why God allowed this or that. On other things we wait a long time to get the explanation. But there is an explanation, and that explanation will come in God's time.

Something happened to me nearly forty years ago that was most painful, and its effect has not left for all these years. I have come to see it as a "thorn in the flesh" (2 Cor. 12:7). Only lately have I seen how good and right this is. God could have told me many years ago but He did not. But lately, I became convinced and have come to see it as possibly the best thing that has ever happened to me. God does not always explain Himself immediately, but I've learned to lower my voice and wait a while. Sooner or later there will be an explanation.

There are, therefore, two categories of people. There are those who aren't happy with the God of the Bible and those who are. Those unhappy with Him like some things. For example, they like the fact that He is loving; they like the fact that He is merciful. But they do not like the fact that He punishes sin, and they understandably do not like it that He lets things happen that aren't very nice. Such people would love to create the "perfect" God. They believe that if they could just change this or just change that, God would then be perfect.

But those who love God as He is believe that He is perfect, that there is nothing about Him that could be improved. And in case you wondered, He did not make Himself perfect; He already was! He did not make Himself like He is; He's always been as He is. He did not say within Himself, "I think I will start being a God of love," or, "From now on I am going to be a God who is all-powerful," or, "From now on I am going to be a God who can be everywhere at the same time—omnipresent." No. God did not decide to be this way. This is just the way He is. And when I've had that aforementioned touch of God on me— and this does not happen every day (although I've had it once in a while), my immediate feeling is (if you can forgive me for putting it like this) I feel that we are lucky that we have a God like that! That is the best way I can put it. I just think, "Wow! You really are like this! This is wonderful!"

KNOWING GOD

The first three of the Ten Commandments are letting us see just a little bit of what God is like. Not that the next seven do not do it, but the first three focus directly on His character, His person. These commands are deep teaching. In a sense they were spoon-feeding Israel, and yet the words are so profound, so deep. Israel was a redeemed community. As we have seen, the word *redeemed* means that they had been bought back. God loved the people of Israel. They knew God, but only just.

How well do you know God? How well would you like to know Him? How deeply is it burning in you that you would love to know Him better? If that desire is there, it means that there is a special anointing—the power of the Holy Spirit—on you. There could be no greater desire on earth. So you can mark it down, the flesh did not put that desire there. The devil did not put that there. This is one desire, if it is there, that only God could put there. And for giving you that kind of thirst and longing, be thankful for it. Take it with both hands and walk in every little bit of light God gives you. Walking in the light will show that you really mean business—that it is not just a passing yearning.

Whenever you discover something that you hadn't seen before, an awareness of sin or a higher level of obedience, take it. There may be that which offends you, but remember that God often tests us by letting us be offended. Sometimes those of us who have had the most violent reaction to something that is supposed to represent God, later find out that we are so glad that we climbed down and changed our tune.

God wants to see how much you want Him. So sometimes, if I may put it this way, He puts His "worst" foot forward; He lets you see the most "unattractive" aspect of His nature, or what He knows you may regard that way, to see whether you will still love Him just as He is.

THE NEED FOR FAITH

The first commandment refers to God's uniqueness, when He said, "You shall have no other gods before me." The second commandment refers to His hiddenness. That is the aspect of God we are looking at in this chapter. So why did God give us this second commandment? The reason is, to make room for faith. "Now faith is being sure of what we hope for and certain of what we do not see" (Heb. 11:1). It is the reason we must have faith in order to please God. "And without faith it is impossible to please God, because anyone who comes to him must believe that he exists and that he rewards those who earnestly seek him" (v. 6). When He decided to make man, God wanted man to love Him. After the Fall of man in the Garden of Eden, He decreed that those who get to know Him will know Him only by faith. This second command shows the reason God must be worshiped by faith.

What then does this mean? Well, you can't see Him, can you? You cannot see God. "God is a spirit, and his worshipers must worship in spirit and in truth" (John 4:24). That means God could be in your room—and He is—and fill the atmosphere—and He's doing it—and yet you can see right through it. He is invisible. He is with you, but you can see right past Him. But an idol is visible. An idol is what you can see, and in a moment it diverts you from looking to God. And God does not like that.

What makes faith, faith is that you rely on God, and yet the only evidence that you have for His existence is His Word. You may ask, "Why on earth would I ever want to believe in His Word?" I can tell you, for those who do, the reward is tremendous. It is endless. He will never leave you. He will never forsake you. He will honor you. He will uphold you. He will never let you down. Using the analogy I used earlier, is it not the highest compliment you can give another person to say that you like them the way they are? Now, would you not also say the highest compliment a person can give you is to believe in your integrity? That they trust you?

If a person does not know me very well, I cannot be justifiably indignant if he wants proof of what I say. He may say, "Let me check this out with someone else, someone that I know." That is fair. I would do the same. But if a person I have known for a long time—who has had no reason to distrust me—begins to question my integrity, I would be perplexed if not a little upset.

When we know God, that He is "good" (1 Pet. 2:3), that He keeps His word, that His promises have proved to be true, and that He never leaves us or forsakes us (Heb. 13:5), He too would be grieved if we began to question His judgment. That is what made Him angry with the children of Israel. After He miraculously delivered them from Pharaoh, they began to grumble against God and Moses. "They spoke against God and against Moses, and said, 'Why have you brought us up out of Egypt to die in the desert? There is no bread! There is no water! And we detest this miserable food!'" (Num. 21:5). These people were without excuse. God had been true and faithful to them.

The Bible is God's integrity put on the line. As for those who believe His Word, He loves that. He not only loves it that you love Him as He is; He also wants you to believe in His integrity. If I say to you that I give you my word, and you say, "Well, that is all I need," you have affirmed me to the hilt. I come from the hills of Kentucky, and our motto is based on the handshake. If you shook hands, it was done. That is because in those days many people couldn't write! So they just shook hands—they couldn't sign a document. That handshake was it. It affirmed one's word. You did not have to sign your name—they believed what you said. But what if we do not even shake hands? I just say, "I believe you. Your word is enough. Your word is your bond. I believe it." That affirms your integrity.

God likes that. So we have that description of faith in Hebrews 11:1. It is very important to remember. For faith to be faith, you can't have the evidence. No proof. It is just God's Word. And you believe that Word.

You say, "Why would anybody do that?" Because the Holy Spirit applies the Word. We sometimes refer to it as effectual calling. "And we also thank God continually because, when you received the word of God, which you heard from us, you accepted it not as the word of men, but as it actually is, the word of God, which is at work in you who believe" (1 Thess. 2:13). Paul said that the gospel he preached came "not simply with words, but also with power, with the Holy Spirit and with deep conviction"

(1 Thess. 1:5). It is when God moves in and makes a person admit to himself or herself, "That is me—this describes me completely." It is a moment of understanding, "when the penny drops," as the British say. One sees for himself or herself that it is really true— Jesus Christ died for our sins and is alive today! It is the Holy Spirit who converts. It is not one's great intellect; it is not education. God applies the Word by the Spirit. God's Word does not return empty (Isa. 55:11). The Holy Spirit applies the Word. None of us has seen God, but some heard the Word and were gripped. They began to see that when they trust Him He keeps His Word. "The one who trusts in him will never be put to shame" (Rom. 9:33).

God honors those who honor Him (1 Sam. 2:30), and the highest way you honor Him is to honor His Word.

One of the hymns I love includes a line about being "among the mockers." One of the things that mockers said at the crucifixion was, "Let this Christ, this King of Israel, come down now from the cross, that we may see and believe" (Mark 15:32). That was the equivalent of idolatry. Wanting to see in order to believe. "Jews demand miraculous signs" (1 Cor. 1:22). That is also what an idol is all about. An idol is something you can see.

The reason this second command demonstrates the hiddenness of God is, however, because of the need for faith. An idol is, therefore, something you can see, but Israel would get impatient. They would say, "Where is this God?" It is amazing they would ask that. He had just delivered them from the bondage of Pharaoh! He had just enabled them to cross the Red Sea on dry land! They saw His power, and yet after a little while, when things did not go perfectly right, they began to murmur and complain, and they wanted to worship an idol. Why? They said, "We want something we can see. We want it before our eyes." For that is what an idol is. It interferes with faith. God wants to be believed on the basis of His Word. Alone.

The irony is, they had seen God work. They were without excuse. It happened after Jesus fed the five thousand with five barley loaves and two small fish (John 6:1–14). They actually insulted Him by saying, "What miraculous sign then will you give that we may see it and believe you?" (John 6:30). The demand to see in order to believe nullified faith in that moment. Faith to be faith means believing without seeing. When God withholds the evidence we claim we want He is doing us a great favor. That is what Jesus did by refusing to grant Mary's and Martha's request to come at once to heal Lazarus. No one understood at the time why He did not move immediately. But He gave the answer: "that you may believe" (John 11:14). That means embracing God's Word and wisdom before we have the empirical evidence. It is that alone that makes faith, faith.

All our worship is to be by faith. Sometimes I do not feel like worshiping—I may be tired, sometimes my mind wanders, sometimes everything went wrong that day. But as the writer of Hebrews puts it, "Let us continually offer to God a sacrifice of praise" (Heb. 13:15). It really is a sacrifice. I am not particularly enjoying it; it is by faith. But one day we are going to worship in heaven. Worship there will be by sight, not faith.

IDOLS

The reason that God said, "You shall not make for yourself an idol," is because an idol interferes with faith, competes with faith, and wars against faith. That is the main reason for this second command.

Another reason, however, is because of God's intolerance for idolatry. An idol is what man created. Sometimes it was made out of wood, sometimes out of stone. Sometimes they would put gold over the wood or over the stone. These idols might point to something in the sky such as the moon or the sun—sometimes people actually worshiped the moon or the sun. They would also make an idol of a bird or something on earth, or even a fish in the sea. Why did they do it? They said, "We want to be able to see it." They also could control it. People can do all the talking; there will be no listening. An idol is helpless. Some people want a God like that, a God whom you can feel sorry for or control.

The God of the Bible can do anything. He's all-powerful; He is not helpless, and He does not even need us.

In Romans 1:25, Paul talked about worshiping the creature "rather than the Creator." God hates that. God is the one who made these things. He wants you to admire them, but not to worship them. He wants you to admire the moon and the stars, the planets, the ocean, the mountains, the beauty of nature. He wants you to admire the way He made you. The psalmist said that we are "fearfully and wonderfully made" (Ps. 139:14). You stand in awe of the way we are made.

But an idol is erected by man, and it diverts us from the true God. That is why the devil is perched on every person's shoulder hoping that one will opt for an idol. An idol is anything that diverts your focus from God. It does not have to be a piece of wood or stone; it is anything that diverts you from focusing upon God.

A JEALOUS GOD

God also wants us to know He is a jealous God. He says so. He's up front about it. Jealousy is not an attractive quality in human beings. You may say, "I do not think it is an attractive quality in God." That is your privilege; that may be one of the things you would like to change about Him. Maybe that is why you feel He needs correcting. But listen to what He says in this second command: "You shall not worship them, for I the LORD your God am a jealous God." He wants you to know that is the way He is. In fact, if you have seen jealousy here below, that is just the tip of the iceberg compared with how jealous jealousy can be. Because God is jealous in an infinite way. A husband may be jealous of his wife or vice versa. You have heard of the jealous lover. Maybe you are jealous of another person's success. Maybe you are jealous of another person's looks or their money, and it just consumes you with hate. Maybe you are jealous of a person, and you just long for their downfall. Nothing would thrill you more than to see somebody crash.

Jealousy is that of which God says, "I am that," and He has a right to be as He is and to tell us about Himself—which He might have hidden. Although He is hidden in the sense that you cannot see Him because He is not physically discerned, He does not hide this aspect of Himself in His words. What this means is that God cannot bear your putting anything before Him. And it just may be that this too is one of the things that you do not like about Him.

Can I tell you why I like it that He's a jealous God? It is because I see that He really cares about what I do. The worst thing in the world is when God does not communicate with us or let us know what offends Him. The worst thing that can happen in war is when your enemy is not known to you and you do not know what he is up to. Martin Luther said we must know God as an enemy before we can know Him as a friend. Not that God really is an enemy, but He can certainly appear to be. And yet His wrath is very real. Paul said we who are saved were, like the rest of the world, "objects of wrath" (Eph. 2:3). He therefore shows His displeasure by hiding His face and letting things go badly wrong with us to get our attention. When that is happening we can truly feel His anger. And yet it is because He loves us so much! But we must never forget that by nature we are at enmity with God. This is why the Bible talks about reconciliation between God and man; God is holy, and we are sinners. God is wholly other—He's out there but different from us. We are creatures. We are frail, and by nature—I say it again—we hate the true God. We do not even like Him a little bit. God could in His anger and wrath not even bother to let us know what He's like. As far as we know, Sodom and Gomorrah got no warning (Gen. 19). God just wiped them off the map. He hated the sin so much, but He did not bother to tell them, did not bother to communicate.

When God bothers to tell you what He is like, and He says "I am a jealous God," you should say, "Thank You for telling me that." I love Him for telling me. And I love that He is that way because it shows how much He loves me. That means that He will go to pains to correct me so that everything He does is for my good. I know what it is to have God put me through strenuous ordeals to get my attention. When I do that which displeases Him and He lets me know, it is a great sign of His jealous care. What He permits can be most painful. And yet everything He permits is for my good. And He does what He has to do to get my attention. And sometimes it hurts, and sometimes I look up to Him with tears rolling down my cheeks and say, "God, why did You do that?" But I know, in time, it was the only way God could get my attention. Like with my "thorn in the flesh." What I once resented I now accept as the best thing that could have happened to me. I cannot reveal what it is, but I can categorically state that I now see the wisdom of God—and jealous care—in it all.

So why is He the way He is? He wants to be believed without the evidence. They said, "Come down from the cross and we will see and then believe." But that is not faith. It is not faith when you see and believe; it is faith when you believe and then see. God has a way of letting us "see"—by confirming our faith—if we wait. "Wait for the LORD; be strong and take heart and wait for the LORD" (Ps. 27:14).

THE JUSTICE AND MERCY OF GOD

God is simultaneously wrath and mercy. Just and merciful. He says so. "I the LORD your God am a jealous God, punishing the children for the sin of the fathers to the third and fourth generation of those who hate me, but showing love to a thousand generations of those who love me and keep my commandments" (Exod. 20:5–6).

God can be summarized in two ways, for the Bible basically tells us two things about God: that He is merciful and that He is just. I love the hymn "Beneath the Cross of Jesus" and especially that line, "O trysting place where heaven's love and heaven's justice meet."[1] That hymn demonstrates this: He is a God of justice; He is a God of love. What then does that mean? It means He's angry with sin, and it means He must punish sin. God does not like it that you have not lived for Him. He does not like it that you have abused your body, the money He's let you have, the life He's given you. And you have let the years go on. And you do not care what He thinks; you have taken things into your own hands—you are an idolater; you want what you can see. You want a God that you can control. You will not have a God who holds your destiny in His hands. And God is angry.

God created hell for the devil and his angels and for all those who side with Satan (Matt. 25:41). However unfair, unjust, and incomprehensible eternal punishment is to us, I guarantee you it will not be a mystery then. God does not always explain Himself in advance. This is why we take Him at His Word and believe it. There are two ways God ultimately punishes sin: by the fires of hell or by the blood of Jesus. There are, likewise, two things the Bible says about God: He's just, but He's also merciful. The latter

91

means He does not want to punish us.

The big question follows, then, how could God be just and merciful at the same time? The answer is, He sent His Son into the world two thousand years ago, who died on a cross. While He was on the cross, all of our sins were transferred to Jesus as though He were guilty. And if you want to know how much God hates sin, I just want you to picture what happened on Good Friday when all of God's wrath was poured out on Jesus, on God's Son! Nobody suffered like that. It was awful. Our sin was on the shoulders of God's Son. And God punished Him for what we did. Not for what Jesus did. Jesus never sinned. "God made him who had no sin to be sin for us, so that in him we might become the righteousness of God" (2 Cor. 5:21).

The way God can be just and merciful at the same time is that His justice was satisfied when Jesus shed His blood. That way He can be merciful to you and me.

GOD'S PROVIDENCE

There is one more thing that we see from this second commandment. It is God's concern for tomorrow's generation: "Punishing the children for the sin of the fathers to the third and fourth generation of those who hate me, but showing love to a thousand generations of those who love me and keep my commandments" (Exod. 20:5–6). Care for tomorrow's generation.

Cain asked the question, "Am I my brother's keeper?" (Gen. 4:9). And by the way, the answer to that is, yes. And we may ask, are we responsible for tomorrow's generation? Yes. It lies within me to make it harder or easier for tomorrow's generation. And if we can honor God and wait before Him and leave a legacy to the next generation, it shows that we care about tomorrow. Man only wants what is "for me." God is concerned about tomorrow, and if we honor Him and love Him we will be concerned about tomorrow. We will care about the future, about what happens to the church, what happens to the honor of God's name.

God is concerned about tomorrow's generation. This was repeated in Exodus 34:6–7: "He passed in front of Moses, proclaiming, 'The LORD, the LORD, the compassionate and gracious God, slow to anger, abounding in love and faithfulness, maintaining love to thousands, and forgiving wickedness, rebellion and sin. Yet He does not leave the guilty unpunished; He punishes the children and their children for the sin of their fathers to the third and fourth generation.'"

We have a duty, as best as we can, to leave a legacy to those who will carry on after we move on.

Chapter 8

THE THIRD COMMANDMENT:
THE NAME OF GOD

You shall not misuse the name of the LORD your
God, for the LORD will not hold anyone guiltless
who misuses his name.

—EXODUS 20:7

A NAME IS A word or words by which one is known. It refers
primarily to one's identity. We identify a person by his or
her name. It is what distinguishes a person from another
individual.

When God revealed Himself to Moses at the burning bush
and announced to him, "I am sending you to Pharaoh to bring
my people the Israelites out of Egypt" (Exod. 3:1–10), Moses soon
wanted to know God's name.

Moses said to God, "Suppose I go to the Israelites and say to
them, 'The God of your fathers has sent me to you,' and they
ask me, 'What is his name?' Then what shall I tell them?"

—EXODUS 3:13

God answered, "I AM WHO I AM. Therefore if anyone asks
who sent you, tell them: 'I AM has sent me to you'" (v. 14). From
this emerged the *tetragrammaton*—the four Hebrew letters

YHWH translated as "the LORD" and considered too sacred to pronounce by some Jews (and Orthodox Jews to this day). When vowels were combined with the consonants YHWH it was once assumed the spelling should be *Jehovah*, a form first attested at the beginning of the twelfth century A.D. Scholarly studies since have shown that the pronunciation should be *Yahweh*, and such is indicated by transliteration of the name into Greek in early Christian literature. There is no indication that ancient Jews did not pronounce the name. Not pronouncing *Yahweh* but substituting *Adonai* was probably a medieval superstition that gave Jews a righteous feeling. Indeed, some might feel they are carrying out the third commandment by not pronouncing *Yahweh*.

The term *God* does not itself give identity. The Hebrew *Elohim* refers to God as a powerful being. It is the first term used in the Bible for Creator God (Gen. 1:1). It is also in the plural in the Hebrew, suggesting the Trinity. This helps explain God's saying, "Let us make man in our image, in our likeness" (Gen. 1:26). *God* is a generic term and does not necessarily imply the Christian view of God. But when we speak of God's name we refer to *Yahweh*. This is the Old Testament word that clearly identifies the name of the true God, that is, the God who made a covenant with His people. He is referred to in the New Testament as the God who sent His Son into the world and is called the God and Father of our Lord Jesus Christ.

One of the most startling verses in the Old Testament is Exodus 6:3. "I appeared to Abraham, to Isaac and to Jacob as God Almighty, but by my name the LORD I did not make myself known to them." How could this be? Did not men in earliest times "call on the name of the LORD" (Gen. 4:26)? Did not Abraham build "an altar to the LORD" and call on "the name of the LORD" (Gen. 12:8)? The explanation consists partly in the probability that they called on that name but did not understand its meaning or feel a need to know God's identity. But Moses needed to know more, and God began to unfold more to Moses.

THE IMPORTANCE OF ONE'S NAME

Name, however, refers not only to one's identity but also to one's reputation. We often refer to a person as having "a good name."

A good name is more desirable than great riches; to be esteemed is better than silver or gold.

—PROVERBS 22:1

Who steals my purse steals trash...
'Twas mine, 'tis his, and has been slave to thousands.
But he that filches from me my good name
Robs me of that which not enriches him,
And makes me poor indeed.[1]

The name of God, that is, His reputation, became an issue in ancient times. When God threatened to destroy the whole people of Israel and start all over again, Moses interceded and pleaded:

If you put these people to death all at one time, the nations who have heard this report about you will say, "The LORD was not able to bring these people into the land he promised them on oath; so he slaughtered them in the desert."

—NUMBERS 14:15–16

When Joshua sent the two spies to Jericho, they met Rahab, who said:

I know that the LORD has given this land to you and that a great fear of you has fallen on us, so that all who live in this country are melting in fear because of you. We have heard how the LORD dried up the water of the Red Sea for you when you came out of Egypt, and what you did to Sihon and Og, the two kings of the Amorites east of the Jordan, whom you completely destroyed. When we heard of it, our hearts melted and everyone's courage failed because of you, for the LORD your God is God in heaven above and on the earth below.

—JOSHUA 2:9–11

God's name was held in high honor, and God wants that to remain. He has unveiled Himself not only as a God who is jealous but also as a God of glory.

97

I am the LORD; that is my name! I will not give my glory to
another or my praise to idols.

—ISAIAH 42:8

The first thing Jesus' disciples were to learn about the Father
in the Lord's Prayer was, "Hallowed be your name" (Matt. 6:9).
Said the psalmist, "Holy and awesome is his name" (Ps. 111:9).

The third commandment was given to protect the honor
of God's name from abuse. One of the most timely and relevant
hymns written in our time is by Graham Kendrick and Chris
Robinson:

Restore, O Lord, the honor of your name...
And in our time revive the church that bears your name,
That men may see and come with reverent fear
To the living God whose kingdom shall outlast the
    years.[2]

The King James Version states Exodus 20:7 this way: "Thou
shalt not take the name of the LORD thy God in vain; for the LORD
will not hold him guiltless that taketh his name in vain." The
phrase "take in vain" comes from a root word meaning "to be
waste," the idea of being empty of meaning.

The people of Israel were therefore being taught, line by line,
to understand God and His ways. When we walk in the Spirit,
in the light of God's Word, we too learn these things. We have
seen that God brought the Ten Commandments to Israel at a
time when they had sinned against Him; it was because of their
sinfulness that God stepped in and introduced the Law, which
would be fulfilled when Jesus died on the cross. By walking in the
Spirit we will keep every one of the commands. And one example
of how we will keep the third command is that our talk about God
will show reverence to His name.

The third command refers mainly to the way we talk
about God. We ought to be aware that God is listening to our
conversations, day and night. He is eavesdropping on every word
we say. One of the most sobering verses in the Bible—it terrifies
me—is, "But I tell you that men will have to give account on the

day of judgment for every careless word they have spoken" (Matt. 12:36). I wish that were not true.

I remember as a boy listening to a radio broadcast called the *Old Fashioned Revival Hour* that came from the tabernacle of Charles Fuller in California. They had a quartet that sang these lines:

> He sees all you do,
> He hears all you say,
> My Lord is a-writin' all the time.
>
> —Anonymous

He keeps records of all that we say or do. And this command has to do with the way people talk about God.

There is a warning in Proverbs: "When words are many, sin is not absent, but he who holds his tongue is wise" (Prov. 10:19). And so, when we talk to each other, if we are not careful, sin will come in at one point—some misunderstanding or hurt feeling. John Wesley gave the advice that people should spend as much time in prayer as they do talking to each other. I wonder what that would do to our fellowship, to the things we say, if we paused and said, "Oops, hour's up—time to pray now for an hour." What that would do to our conversations!

"You shall not misuse the name of the LORD your God." The Hebrew may be translated, "Do not use His name with no purpose." This was to warn a person about entering into conversation about God in a casual manner. And so, we must not want to take God's name in vain, that is, we do not want merely to start talking about God casually. In a word, this commandment has to do with respecting God's character, but with particular reference to His name. And so, God teaches us about His name. He cares about His name.

Do you care about your name? If you notice an article somewhere and your name might be in it, whose name do you look for first? Or how do you like it if somebody mispronounces your name? Or misspells your name? Sometimes we try to "get another person's goat"—this is not something we ought to do—merely by slightly mispronouncing their name. I knew somebody who used to say, "Hello, Kendarl"—he knew I did not like that. There was a student in my high school years who would call me "HQ." Long ago, Martin Luther had an argument with Zwingli of Zurich, and sadly he wouldn't call him "Zwingli"; he called him "Zwingle." It is a way of putting a person down. We care about our names.

I remember talking to a man who worked as an intern in a mental hospital. He was there as a chaplain. He said there was one old lady who would walk up and down the corridors all day long, saying, "Is there anyone here who knows my name? Is there anyone here who knows my name?" We all care about our names. And so God's name is important to Him. And He does us no favor not to tell us that, because He says, "The LORD will not hold anyone guiltless who misuses his name" (Exod. 20:7).

All of us are favored—blessed—with the knowledge of God's name....God is giving us the highest privilege on Earth, and that is to know Him.

In the Old Testament, a person's name was loaded with meaning. It not only was an identification so that you would say "John" or "Mary"—knowing who the person was; often the name was an index into his or her character. Or it would pertain to the mission that they had. Many times God would tell what to name the child. In fact, God told Joseph what to name the baby that would be born of Mary. "She will give birth to a son, and you are to give him the name Jesus, because he will save his people from their sins" (Matt. 1:21). And if you translate the Greek back into Hebrew it comes out Joshua. The word *Joshua* means "Deliverer." Jacob's name was changed to Israel because Israel means "one who struggles with God," and Jacob had wrestled with the angel. So an Old Testament person's name is a guide to that person's character. We are told, then, in Exodus 6:3—one of the most extraordinary verses—that God said, "I appeared to Abraham, to Isaac and to Jacob as God Almighty, but by my name the LORD I did not make myself known to them."

This allows us to see that when God was prepared to reveal His name, it was a most high privilege for Israel. All of us are favored—blessed—with the knowledge of God's name. Even to Abraham, Isaac, and Jacob, He did not unfold His name. But

He did to Moses. And He did to the people of Israel. And He's doing it now. And He comes to us with the offering of a personal relationship with Him. God is giving us the highest privilege on Earth, and that is to know Him.

"FOLK RELIGION"

It seems that, with everything God does, when something great takes place there also emerges a "folk religion" that enables people who aren't that interested in God's heartbeat nonetheless to get a religious feeling. Some Jews get that when they piously substitute *Adonai* for *Yahweh* when they pray or refer to God.

What is "folk religion"? It is having enough religion to make you feel religious without it changing your life. That is what it comes to. Every Christian denomination has its own brand of folk religion. It may be theological jargon that coheres with one's "comfort zone." It may be a certain tone of voice that identifies one's background, especially when one prays publicly. It may be a style of oratory in preaching that purports to be the "anointing." It may be the style of worship, the sound of guitars or the pipe organ. Some think they are more spiritual because the women wear hats. Some put a high priority on the manner in which the Lord's Supper is carried out. Some feel it is godlier to use the King James Version—in public and private. I could go on and on. In contemporary Israel they have their own kind of folk religion, as not to pronounce the name *Yahweh*. Why? They say God's name is too holy to pronounce. So that gives them a religious feeling. It does not have any effect on their lives. The fact that you have a respect for the name of God in that way—some Jews wouldn't even write it, unless they would take a different pen, use a different ink; it too gave them a religious feeling—this is not what God wants.

WRONG USE OF GOD'S NAME

I want to show what it means to abuse God's name. It largely comes down to one thing, and that is using His name to make yourself look good. That is a sure way to abuse His name. The right use of the name of God is when you make Him look good and you focus on Him, when your whole purpose in talking about Him is to focus on Him. But when you "name-drop" God's name, you are really focusing on yourself. You are trying to make yourself look good. God does not like it, not one little bit. And He promises He will not hold anyone guiltless who misuses His name to make themselves look good.

In the Sermon on the Mount Jesus interpreted this third commandment almost with throwaway comments. It was not a whole exposition of it, but He referred to the third commandment implicitly when He said:

> Again, you have heard that it was said to the people long ago, "Do not break your oath, but keep the oaths you have made to the LORD." But I tell you, Do not swear at all: either by heaven, for it is God's throne; or by the earth, for it is his footstool; or by Jerusalem, for it is the city of the Great King. And do not swear by your head, for you cannot make even one hair white or black. Simply let your "Yes" be "Yes," and your "No," "No"; anything beyond this comes from the evil one.
>
> —MATTHEW 5:33–37

In ancient times, the third commandment applied to making a vow or "promising on oath." When one promised on oath it was to ensure that the promise certainly would be carried out. Or if one appealed to a greater authority—God's name, for example—it was to guarantee what one affirmed. In Hebrews 6 we get a clear picture of the nature and purpose of an oath. First, one always appealed to "someone greater than themselves"—God, heaven, or the angels— and, second, its aim was to put an end to all argument (v. 16). It was thought to be perfectly legitimate to promise on oath—and appeal to God's name—as long as you were telling the truth and would keep your vow (Num. 30:2; Deut. 23:21). For the Lord would not hold anyone guiltless who misused His name. Once Yahweh's name was invoked, the vow to which it was attached became a debt that had to be paid to the Lord. You did not misuse God's name as long as you kept your word. You only misused His name if you lied or broke your promise.

But Jesus was going beyond this in His interpretation and

application of the third command. He says, "Do not swear at all." In other words, do not bring in any higher authority to vindicate yourself or endear yourself. Just tell the truth—simply: "Let your 'Yes' be 'Yes,' and your 'No,' 'No.'" What is more, do not bring God's name in at all; leave Him out. For when you appeal to His name to make yourself believable or trustworthy, the devil himself gets in.

The point was that people, in order to elevate their own credibility, would swear by the name of God. Why did they do that? They did that in order to be believed. They would make themselves look better. I might say, "I really am telling you the truth." It suggests that I had not really told the truth until then! I fear I do it all the time. I will say, "I really do mean this." I am afraid one will not believe me, so I add words like that. Now talking like that has not misused God's name—yet. But the temptation often comes to appeal to a higher authority if I fear I am not being believed. I might say, "If I am totally honest"; I do so to get another's attention. No sin here, I suppose. But if I say, "God knows I am telling the truth," I have crossed over the line. I am not making God look good, only myself. I have crossed over the line.

Whenever we swear we look for a higher authority, so that the other person will believe we are really telling the truth. Sometimes a person will say, "I swear by God," or "I swear on my mother's grave." This would be "swearing by earth." You try to appeal to something that will make the other person think, "Ah, you really are telling the truth." So in ancient Israel they would swear by the name of God to say, "I am telling the truth." They were not thinking of God; they were thinking of themselves. They were focusing on themselves; they wanted themselves to look credible. And Jesus said, "Don't even do that." In fact, He said, "Don't swear by anything. Just let your word be it. If you say it, that is it."

Some have taken this to mean that a person should not swear in a court of law. That is altogether different; this has no relevance to a court of law. When you are required to do something under fear of perjury, you should obey the law. There is nothing wrong with a person doing that. Otherwise, God would not have encouraged one to do it in ancient times: "Fear the LORD your God, serve him only and take your oaths in his name" (Deut. 6:13).

The reason for the third commandment and the reason for

Jesus' way of applying it in the Sermon on the Mount was so that a person would not abuse the name of the Lord, just "using" His name.

James had Jesus' statement in the Sermon on the Mount in mind when He referred to people in the early church, a group of poor Christians who worked for rich Christians who did not pay their wages (James 5:1–12). How would you feel if you worked for a Christian who did not pay you your salary? If they only said, "Sorry about that, we will pay you a little bit next week," you would think, *Well, this is not right; this is not fair.* And you would think, *I thought these were Christians, and I have to feed my family.* That was actually happening; that is what James talks about. He says to rich Christians: "The wages you failed to pay the workmen who mowed your fields are crying out against you. The cries of the harvesters have reached the ears of the Lord Almighty" (v. 4). God knew they were being mistreated.

James first warned the rich Christians who did not pay the wages that the laborers deserved. But then he shifted his address to the poor Christians. He warned them and said, "Above all, do not swear" (v. 12). He was then talking to those who had been abused. He knew they would be tempted severely to bring in God's name. After all, when you are mistreated and hurt, you become desperate. And before you know it, you bring God in and say, "God does not like what you are doing. God is going to deal with you for that. God is upset with you, and you are going to be in real trouble, because God does not like it." Why would one do that? He or she brings God in to create fear. But you are thinking not of God; you are thinking of yourself.

James knew the temptation that these Christians would have to do that, and we have all done this I suppose—I know I have. And I've seen how wrong it is, and I tell you, I've had more than just a slap on the wrist from God for doing it. He does not like it, even if I am wronged. And James was saying to these Christians who were abused, "Look, God is on your side; He is with you. He knows what they have done to you, but do not bring His name in." Don't "name-drop" God. Keep Him out of it. Don't bolster your case by saying He is on your side and not theirs.

Do you know what it is to be a name-dropper? How many

of us love name-droppers? Why do we name-drop? To make ourselves look good. To let others know that we know somebody, especially if they are well known. We do it to make another person feel a little envious of us, so they will treat us with more respect. But what we are doing is using that person's name. We are not trying to make them look good; we are trying to make ourselves look good. And you see, God does not like it when we bring in His name for a personal reason out of self-interest. So the third command comes to this: do not use God's name. Don't name-drop God.

The right use of God's name is when you are trying to make Him look good, and you are focusing upon Him. We all can tell, if we are honest with ourselves, whether—when we refer to God—we are making Him look good or ourselves look good. I always worry about that person who, when they come to me, before you know it, they are talking about the Lord who "is so precious to me. He's so real to me." "The Lord said this to me." "The Lord told me to do this." There are people like that who just want to make themselves look good by bringing His name in. "The Lord has told me this." Really? Why do we need to say so?

The right use of God's name is to worship Him. The psalmist, for example, when he would bring in the name of the Lord, would never, never, never do it to make himself look good. Rather, he would say, "Glorify the LORD with me, let us exalt his name together" (Ps. 34:3).

Our responsibility is to proclaim God and make Him look good. So the right use of God's name is focusing on Him for His sake. When we equate the name of Jesus with Yahweh, we are making Jesus look good, and we are making Yahweh look good. Yahweh gave to Jesus the name that is above every name (Phil. 2:9). Yahweh wants Jesus to be called God—for He is the Lord, He reigns on high, and He is God Almighty. This Jesus is Yahweh become flesh, the God-man. He is the one who went to the cross and was despised and hated, who shed His blood but was raised from the dead. God highly exalted Him so that all who call upon the name of the Lord will be saved. If you ask God to forgive your sins in Jesus' name today, you will be saved. For He is God. That is the right use of His name.

Our praying is to be in Jesus' name. The miracles, the healings, are the result of the power of Jesus' name, because God's name and His power come together. God did not reveal His name to Abraham, Isaac, and Jacob (Exod. 6:3), but at the moment when God unveiled His name to Moses, signs, wonders, and miracles began to take place. Power is in the name of God. But He does not want His name abused. The wrong use of God's name is when I vindicate myself by using His name. If I were to tell you, "God is on my side but not on the side of my critics or my enemies," God would look down from heaven with anger. God will not hold me guiltless.

For a further example, let us say that a husband and wife get into an argument. He will say, "God does not like what you just did." And that supposedly means that the husband is really hearing from the Lord and the poor wife has to say, "Oh well, God is against me." In the husband and wife relationship, if that sort of thing ever creeps in, God says, "I am out of it." And all suffer: the husband for his misuse and abuse of God's name, the wife who fears God is angry with her, and God Himself whose name was just "used."

It grieves God to imply that He is for you but against your enemy. Never do that. If you do that, God will turn on you, not your enemy! Do not use His name to make yourself look good!

Jesus said, "Do not even swear in His name." I was brought up to believe, rightly or wrongly, that this commandment referred to swearing, that is, using bad language. It certainly does include that. In fact, anybody walking in the Spirit will not say, "Oh, Jesus. Oh, Christ." Cursing. "Oh my God." You will not do that in the Spirit.

I am indebted to Brian Edwards for pointing out that in the ninth edition of the Concise Oxford Dictionary (1995), the first entry for the word "Jesus" reads: "An exclamation of surprise, dismay, etc." Added to this in square brackets: "Name of the founder of the Christian religion, d. c. A.D. 30." In other words, if one only had this to go by, Jesus is merely to be understood as a swear word—and only secondarily as the one who founded Christianity.[3]

Blaspheming therefore is a blatant example of how God's name can be misused. Years ago when Arthur Blessitt was first at

Westminster Chapel, I remember a young lady who was converted. I happened to know who she was—and she came forward at the end of the service. I was told later that on her way home she said, "Oh my God," and she said, "Ooops—I can't say that!" Do you know, no one told her not to say that, but she had just gone forward that evening. And it showed the Spirit; as soon as she started to fall into a bad habit, she was convicted. Because when you walk in the Spirit, you will not use language like that.

But another way we misuse God's name is to break a confidence when God confides in us. Psalm 25:14 says, "The LORD confides in those who fear him." The King James Version reads, "The secret of the LORD is with them that fear him." God may confide in you. If He does, that may mean you are not to tell it. Sometimes when something special happens to us, we want to tell just one person. There is a place for sharing, of course. As Paul says, "Rejoice with those who rejoice; mourn with those who mourn" (Rom. 12:15), so we need to share with someone when we are sad. And yet it is easier to find someone to weep with you than to rejoice with you. And I am sure we need to have someone to rejoice with us at times. But I do think it would be a real test of one's spirituality to keep a special manifestation of God to oneself. "How can you believe if you accept praise from one another, yet make no effort to obtain the praise that comes from the only God?" (John 5:44). In much the same vein, how many of us could have tea with the queen of England and keep quiet about it? And how many of us could receive a word from the Lord that was just for us and keep quiet about it? The Lord is looking for fellowship. He wants somebody who fears Him and has such respect for His name that He can confide in them, knowing that they will not say, "Oh, look what the Lord told me today. I was just talking to Him, and the Lord said this and the Lord said that." This is the very thing that God does not want.

There can be a kind of folk religion among Christians where it would seem quite right to say, "Well, the Lord said this to me." But how often, if you use that phrase, are you trying to make God look good? Or is it to make you look good? You are using His name. Whenever you say, "The Lord gave me this word," or "The Lord told me this," ask yourself if this is going to make God look good or make you look good. That is the test.

Recently I was preparing a sermon that I knew would be controversial. I feared that my most ardent supporters might have trouble believing I was expounding a particular text correctly. I wondered to myself, *How can I make them see that this really is what God wants said?* I had an idea: I will say that this is true "before God and the angels"—that will get their attention and make them embrace this word. But no. I could not do that. I remembered Jesus' admonition against swearing by heaven or earth in Matthew 5:34–35. It is not that I would have been swearing. But I was bringing in God and the angels to bolster my interpretation—to make it look good. I dropped the idea and hoped that God would be pleased to grant more power by simple talk. For Jesus said, "Simply let your 'Yes' be 'Yes,' and your 'No,' 'No'; anything beyond this comes from the evil one" (v. 37). Doing more than that is, to quote Shakespeare, "protesting too much."

"The LORD will not hold him guiltless." I know what it is to abuse this word. I know what it is to grieve the Holy Spirit in my impatience, but God has never bent the rules for me. I will get egg on my face every time when I try to bring in something that is confidential between God and me to try to impress another person. God will probably use somebody else other than myself.

Whenever we "use" God's name, He will pass us by and find somebody who will have so much respect for His name that even in conversation when they refer to Him, they only want Him to look good.

Chapter 9

THE FOURTH COMMANDMENT:
IS SUNDAY SPECIAL?

Remember the Sabbath day by keeping it holy.
Six days you shall labor and do all your work,
but the seventh day is a Sabbath to the LORD
your God. On it you shall not do any work,
neither you, nor your son or daughter, nor your
manservant or maidservant, nor your animals,
nor the alien within your gates. For in six days
the LORD made the heavens and the earth, the
sea, and all that is in them, but he rested on the
seventh day. Therefore the LORD blessed the
Sabbath day and made it holy.

—EXODUS 20:8–11

P OPE CALLS ON Catholics to Defend Sabbath" was a headline
in Britain's *Daily Telegraph* on July 4, 1998. Pope John Paul
II had issued a high-profile document in which he told
Roman Catholics to respect and defend the Sabbath. He had
often publicly called for Sunday to be a day free of work and one
dedicated to worship, relaxation, and family. In Vienna the pope
told Roman Catholics: "Do whatever you can to protect Sunday.
Make it clear that this day must not be worked, since it must be
celebrated as the day of our Lord."

Reformed Protestantism has historically taken a high view
of what became known as the Christian Sabbath. John Calvin
wrote, "We are not celebrating it [Sunday] as a ceremony with
most rigid scrupulousness. Rather, we are using it as a remedy
needed to keep order in the church for the hearing of the Word,
the administration of the sacraments, and for public prayer."[1] It
is written in the Westminster Confession: "This Sabbath is then
kept holy unto the Lord when men, after a due preparing of their

hearts, and ordering of their common affairs beforehand, do not only observe a holy rest all the day from their own works, and thoughts about their worldly employments and recreations, but also are taken up the whole time in the public and private exercises of his worship, and in the duties of necessity and mercy."[2]

I was brought up in a home that strictly observed Sunday as a day of rest. We were not allowed to do anything on Sunday that was fun or that brought any kind of pleasure. I had a job of delivering newspapers in my teenage years in Ashland, Kentucky. I had 120 customers and had to deliver the *Daily Independent* every evening as well as Sunday mornings. My dad said that the latter was all right because "the ox was in the ditch"—alluding to verses such as Luke 14:5. So I had to work on Sunday mornings to deliver my newspapers. It happened, though, that when I got home, having delivered the Sunday newspaper to our home (because we were on my paper route), lo and behold, my dad always hid our paper! I used to look for the secret place where he had hidden that Sunday newspaper. His best place was behind our piano. I would find it, read it, and put it back so that he wouldn't know I had read it. Never mind that a Monday paper began to be printed on Sunday. We could read the Monday paper! Never mind that the Sunday paper, which we couldn't read, was printed on Saturday. But we could read the Sunday paper on Monday!

Neither could I play basketball in my own backyard, which was the place where all the neighbors wanted to come. My dad had built this beautiful basketball court, which enabled me to learn how to play basketball and become good at it. But we did not use it on Sundays. The kids of the neighborhood were not allowed to come and use my basketball court on Sundays.

I could not do anything fun on Sundays unless a friend of mine invited me to dinner at his house and then, unknown to my dad, we would play some baseball. I do not think my dad ever knew that I did that on Sunday afternoons.

ORIGINS OF THE SABBATH

Some Christian movements have insisted that the Sabbath, the seventh day of the week, remained unchanged by God's statutes from the beginning of Christianity. It is pointed out that the Sabbath was upheld by ancient Judaism, including during the time of our Lord's ministry. Moreover, Paul continued to go into synagogues on the Sabbath (Acts 13:14). After all, there is no explicit verse that suggests the ancient Sabbath (seventh day, which we call Saturday) was changed to Sunday. The Seventh-day Adventist Church is noted for their observation of the seventh-day Sabbath. The Worldwide Church of God (founded by Herbert W. Armstrong) maintains keeping of the seventh-day Sabbath. There are Baptists who keep the seventh-day Sabbath. The common view, therefore, of those who maintain the observance of the seventh day when summed up is: first, ancient Christians went to church on Saturday, and second, the change of the day came because Constantine (c. A.D. 313) changed the day of worship from Saturday to Sunday.

All the above revolves around the fourth commandment. This meant that the period from sunset on Friday to sunset on Saturday was to be kept. This is when the Sabbath is observed in Israel today. Soon after 3:00 p.m., buses return to the terminals, airplanes cease landing at airports, and most shops close down, especially where Orthodox Judaism prevails. Some Orthodox Jews have their electricity turned off, and some do not answer the phone.

There are a few Christians, especially in Scotland, who keep Sunday much like these Jews keep Saturday (except that they tend to date Sunday from midnight Saturday rather than sunset). Some would not eat in a restaurant on Sunday. They would not take a Sunday newspaper (although, as I said, it is printed on Saturday) but take a Monday paper (though it is printed on Sunday). They would not buy an ice cream cone on Sunday. Some do their cooking on Saturdays and only warm the food up on Sundays (though the Law says there can be no lighting of a fire on the Sabbath [Exod. 35:3]).

The ancient Law is clear:

> Observe the Sabbath, because it is holy to you. Anyone who desecrates it must be put to death; whoever does any work on that day must be cut off from his people. For six days, work is to be done, but the seventh day is a Sabbath

111

of rest, holy to the LORD. Whoever does any work on the
Sabbath day must be put to death.

—EXODUS 31:14–15

Until recent years Sunday has been special in Britain—and
it still is in many ways. It was illegal for some shops to be open on
Sundays, but the laws have changed. "Keep Sunday Special" has
been a campaign for some Christians in recent years. In America,
where there is a so-called "Bible Belt," laws that kept shops closed
on Sunday were changed years ago. (It has apparently not hurt
church attendance.)

The issues we raise are: Is Sunday special? Does the New
Testament require that Christians keep the Sabbath? Does the
New Testament suggest that Sunday became the new Sabbath? Is
the so-called Christian Sabbath to be kept as Saturday was kept in
ancient Israel? Is there a biblical case for keeping Sunday special?

We must ask further questions in this chapter. For example,
in the light of our long Christian tradition we should ask—and try
to answer—Is Sunday special? Was Constantine right to change
Christian worship to Sunday? Is the New Testament clear on the
subject? Finally, are Christians obliged to observe Sunday as the
Jews observed Saturday?

It is interesting that the fourth commandment says:
"Remember the Sabbath day." What was to be remembered? That
God rested on the seventh day. God took six days to create the
world and all life. On the seventh day He rested.

By the seventh day God had finished the work he had
been doing; so on the seventh day he rested from all his
work. And God blessed the seventh day and made it holy,
because on it he rested from all the work of creating that
he had done.

—GENESIS 2:2–3

The first hint of keeping the Sabbath is the Israelites'
instruction to gather extra manna. "On the sixth day they are to
prepare what they bring in, and that is to be twice as much as they
gather on the other days" (Exod. 16:5). They were preparing for

the seventh day, the Sabbath, because the Law would require that it be kept, a special day that would be kept to the hilt, to the fullest. "This is what the LORD commanded: 'Tomorrow is to be a day of rest, a holy Sabbath to the LORD. So bake what you want to bake and boil what you want to boil. Save whatever is left and keep it until morning'" (v. 23).

The remembering, therefore, goes back to what Moses was given in Exodus 16. The foundation for this was the order of Creation—that God rested on the Sabbath. But it was not institutionalized until a few days before Sinai. There is no evidence that Noah, Abraham, Isaac, or Jacob kept the Sabbath; it came in with Moses.

The Sabbath was to be kept holy. It was a requirement. Work of every kind by anybody who labored was stopped. It began at sunset on Friday. You could only walk so far; it was called a "Sabbath day's journey." In Acts 1:12 we read: "Then they returned to Jerusalem from the hill called the Mount of Olives, a Sabbath day's walk from the city." This would be about half of a mile. Any kind of a long walk, even if for refreshment, was not allowed.

Even the slaves and animals must stop working. Any visitor who happened to be present must respect the Sabbath. "But the seventh day is a Sabbath to the LORD your God. On it you shall not do any work, neither you, nor your son or daughter, nor your manservant or maidservant, nor your animals, nor the alien within your gates" (Exod. 20:10). This pattern was carried out in a yearly cycle for Israel's farmland (Exod. 23:10–11). In the seventh year you could not grow crops in the same area. The land itself needed rest. And this, of course, is a very healthy thing. Any farmer knows that land needs to rest and not be disturbed by having to grow corn year after year after year after year without some stop. And so there were six years they would grow crops and a year just to let the land rest.

Why did God do this? He did this for man. He did this for His creation. He did this for us. It was a reminder, a requirement; it was rest, that is, of the body: no work—it was enforced rest. This was not for the sake of the Sabbath. Here is where people go wrong. This is where the ancient Jews went wrong. They wanted to glorify the Sabbath, and it was Jesus who came along and said,

"But man was not made for the Sabbath; the Sabbath was made for man." The purpose of all this was for man. It was for the whole of creation. It was an enforced rest—or man would never do it on his own.

The Jews in Jesus' day, especially the Pharisees, focused on the Sabbath. It is interesting to note that the greatest enemies of Jesus were strict Sabbatarians. The probable reasons for this were because one could keep the Sabbath and feel good about oneself; it did not require any change of heart, and it was also a way of making one feel righteous.

The Pharisees were selective with God's commands.

> Then some Pharisees and teachers of the law came to Jesus from Jerusalem and asked, "Why do your disciples break the tradition of the elders? They do not wash their hands before they eat!" Jesus replied, "And why do you break the command of God for the sake of your tradition? For God said, 'Honor your father and mother' and 'Anyone who curses his father or mother must be put to death.' But you say that if a man says to his father or mother, 'Whatever help you might otherwise have received from me is a gift devoted to God,' he is not to 'honor his father' with it. Thus you nullify the word of God for the sake of your tradition. You hypocrites! Isaiah was right when he prophesied about you: 'These people honor me with their lips, but their hearts are far from me. They worship me in vain; their teachings are but rules taught by men.'"
>
> —MATTHEW 15:1–9

The Ten Commandments required a righteousness—outward and inward—that was to be manifested every day. The Pharisees were strict about the Sabbath; they selected this commandment because they felt righteous in keeping it, as if it made up for all other deficiencies.

JESUS AND THE SABBATH

Jesus consciously chose the Sabbath day to perform some of His most extraordinary miracles. One can even guess that any time Jesus saw somebody who needed healing, He said to Himself, "I am going to save that one for the Sabbath!" Why did Jesus choose the Sabbath to perform so many miracles? First, to show that He is Lord of the Sabbath.

> But Jesus knew what they were thinking and said to the man with the shriveled hand, "Get up and stand in front of everyone." So he got up and stood there.
>
> —LUKE 6:8

Second, to expose the hypocrisy of the Pharisees.

> Then Jesus said to them, "I ask you, which is lawful on the Sabbath: to do good or to do evil, to save life or to destroy it?"
>
> —LUKE 6:9

Third, to show the real reason for the Sabbath.

> Then he said to them, "The Sabbath was made for man, not man for the Sabbath."
>
> —MARK 2:27

Jesus wanted to show that once we become legalistic about Sabbath observance—thinking that man was made to glorify the Sabbath—we have missed the point. God gave it because we all need a day of rest.

Have you ever thought about some of Jesus' miracles done on the Sabbath? He healed the man with the shriveled hand (Matt. 12:9–14; Luke 6:6–11). He healed the invalid at the pool of Bethesda (John 5:1–13). He healed the man who was born blind (John 9:1–34). He healed the crippled woman (Luke 13:10–17). He healed the man who suffered from dropsy (Luke 14:1–6).

Never forget that Jesus kept the Sabbath, but not the embellished traditions added on by people such as the Pharisees.

He kept it because He had to keep it. He came to fulfill the Law (Matt. 5:17). The Sabbath was part of the Law.

What Jesus refused to do was to keep the tradition of the elders. The Jews had embellished their understanding of the Sabbath. They went beyond the Law.

> Indignant because Jesus had healed on the Sabbath, the synagogue ruler said to the people, "There are six days for work. So come and be healed on those days, not on the Sabbath."
>
> —LUKE 13:14

The irony is that Jesus went beyond the Law by saying that "hate" is murder; "lusting" is adultery (Matt. 5:21–30). The Jews went beyond the Law by adding their own restrictions about the Sabbath.

There was nothing wrong with healing on the Sabbath. There is nothing in the Law or the Old Testament against it. Jesus only broke the tradition of the elders. For example:

> At that time Jesus went through the grainfields on the Sabbath. His disciples were hungry and began to pick some heads of grain and eat them. When the Pharisees saw this, they said to him, "Look! Your disciples are doing what is unlawful on the Sabbath."
>
> He answered, "Have not you read what David did when he and his companions were hungry? He entered the house of God, and he and his companions ate the consecrated bread—which was not lawful for them to do, but only for the priests. Or haven't you read in the Law that on the Sabbath the priests in the temple desecrate the day and yet are innocent?"
>
> —MATTHEW 12:1–5

He humiliated and infuriated His critics. "Then he asked them, 'If one of you has a son or an ox that falls into a well on the Sabbath day, will you not immediately pull him out?' And they had nothing to say" (Luke 14:5–6). When He healed on the Sabbath, they were "furious" (Luke 6:11). After healing a crippled woman He said, "'Then should not this woman, a daughter of Abraham, whom Satan has kept bound for eighteen long years, be set free on the Sabbath day from what bound her?' When he said this, all his opponents were humiliated, but the people were delighted with all the wonderful things he was doing" (Luke 13:16–17).

A SPECIAL DAY

When I came into a knowledge of sovereign grace more than forty years ago, I felt the most unusual emancipation when I read the Bible and tried to square Scripture with the practice in which I was brought up. I began to realize that our keeping Sunday was a far cry from the way the Jews kept Saturday. Because if you were really going to keep the Sabbath, you would turn off your electricity. I remember meeting Rabbi Abraham Kellner in Washington DC and becoming friendly with him. They would turn off their electricity from outside the house before sunset on Friday, and not until after sunset on Saturday would they go and turn it on. They would not even use a telephone. I am telling you, they kept the Sabbath! I do not know of any Christian who keeps it quite like that.

Then I began to think, "Either we are going to keep it or we are not. Do it like they did it, or do not pretend." There is the feeling that, surely, we just show some respect for it. I have some sympathy with that. But what I began to discover is that in the Book of Acts, the earliest history of the Christian church, there is not a single mention of the Jewish Sabbath to show that Christians observed it. There is only one reference that comes close, and that is in Acts 20:7, which says: "On the first day of the week we came together to break bread." We do not know if that was universal, we do not know if they did it every week, but the Sunday Paul was there they broke bread. This is surely a hint that Christians did not worry about keeping the seventh day. But they apparently observed the first day in some way, because in 1 Corinthians 16:2 Paul said, "On the first day of every week, each one of you should set aside a sum of money in keeping with his income, saving it up, so that when I come no collections will have to be made."

The Sabbath is never mentioned in the New Testament in terms of what Christians are to keep. Consider the times the Ten Commandments are quoted. Jesus said, "Obey the commandments," and then in answer to "Which ones are to be obeyed?" He replied:

> "Do not murder, do not commit adultery, do not steal, do not give false testimony, honor your father and mother," and "love your neighbor as yourself."
>
> —MATTHEW 19:18–19; SEE ALSO MARK 10:19

From Paul:

> The commandments, "Do not commit adultery," "Do not murder," "Do not steal," "Do not covet," and whatever other commandment there may be, are summed up in this one rule: "Love your neighbor as yourself." Love does no harm to its neighbor. Therefore love is the fulfillment of the law.
>
> —ROMANS 13:9–10

From James:

> If you really keep the royal law found in Scripture, "Love your neighbor as yourself," you are doing right. But if you show favoritism, you sin and are convicted by the law as lawbreakers. For whoever keeps the whole law and yet stumbles at just one point is guilty of breaking all of it. For he who said, "Do not commit adultery," also said, "Do not murder." If you do not commit adultery but do commit murder, you have become a lawbreaker.
>
> —JAMES 2:8–11

What is never once mentioned or even implied: the fourth commandment. Is it not strange that it is not even quoted? Must there not be a reason for this?

Jesus was raised from the dead on the first day of the week. All four Gospels testify to this (Matt. 28:1; Mark 16:1–2; Luke 24:1; John 20:1).

118

This day was special to the early church, as we saw above. At least on one occasion the Lord's Supper was celebrated on the "first day of the week" (Acts 20:7), and I refer again to a pattern of giving prescribed with reference to the first day of the week (1 Cor. 16:2).

This probably became known as "the Lord's Day" (Rev. 1:10). Some think, however, that this reference is inconclusive; the Greek is literally translated "day of the Lord." Therefore some think this was John's way of describing the Eschatological Day, that is, his vision of the time of the Lord's Second Coming.

But what is obvious is that Jesus was raised from the dead on the first day of the week, and that made Sunday special. In 1 Corinthians 15:20 the apostle Paul said, "Christ has indeed been raised from the dead, the firstfruits of those who have fallen asleep." *Firstfruits* refers to the resurrection of Jesus. In Leviticus 23:11 we have the account of the feast called "Firstfruits."

> The LORD said to Moses, "Speak to the Israelites and say to them: 'When you enter the land I am going to give you and you reap its harvest, bring to the priest a sheaf of the first grain you harvest. He is to wave the sheaf before the LORD so that it will be accepted on your behalf; the priest is to wave it on the day after the Sabbath.'"
>
> —LEVITICUS 23:9–11

The day after the Sabbath—meaning the first day of the week—shows, at least implicitly, a prophecy that Jesus would be raised on the first day of the week. And that is why the apostle Paul could say Jesus was the firstfruits of the resurrection of the dead.

The Day of Pentecost was on the first day of the week. This is very significant because it shows how the Holy Spirit came down on the day that commemorated the giving of the Law at Sinai, fifty days after Passover. So if we walk in the Spirit, we will fulfill the Law. This is why Paul said, "But if you are led by the Spirit, you are not under law" (Gal. 5:18).

The point is, the seventh-day Sabbath was abolished. It was over. It was finished. The first day became special. But as to whether the first day was to be kept as the seventh day had been kept is another question.

Jesus promised to fulfill the Law (Matt. 5:17), and He fulfilled the keeping of the Sabbath as our substitute. He not only died for us, but in doing so He also fulfilled the Law for us. When we trust Him we are given credit for having fulfilled the Law, as though we kept it. This includes the Sabbath.

When the Spirit came down on the Day of Pentecost, this was as real as Jesus' ministry being personally carried out. For it was Jesus who directed the entire event from God's right hand. As I said, Pentecost was also the commemoration of the Law. The worship of God as a seventh-day act was abolished from that moment.

But as we should live lives that demonstrate the righteousness of the Law (following Jesus), should we not also keep the Sabbath? I partly answer: there is no word in the New Testament about this, although there is about the rest of the Ten Commandments. The reason Paul and others went to synagogues on the Sabbath was to take advantage of the presence of Jews in order to present the gospel. The two references to the first day of the week (Acts 20:7; 1 Cor. 16:2) say nothing about doing no work. Most likely all Christians had to work on Sunday in those days.

Paul warned about a judgmental spirit and the observance of days:

> Therefore do not let anyone judge you by what you eat or drink, or with regard to a religious festival, a New Moon celebration or a Sabbath day. These are a shadow of the things that were to come; the reality, however, is found in Christ.
>
> —COLOSSIANS 2:16–17

> One man considers one day more sacred than another; another man considers every day alike. Each one should be fully convinced in his own mind. He who regards one day as special, does so to the Lord.
>
> —ROMANS 14:5–6

Romans 14:5 is a rather extraordinary verse; I reckon that no Sabbatarian could have made this comment. Moreover, this verse categorically sets aside the legality of a day that must be observed as the ancient Sabbath was observed.

Sabbatarianism often plays into self-righteous feelings, where we can feel good about ourselves and keep it. For some it would be some other observance. I will share what I think is a funny story. I told this publicly at Westminster Chapel when Dr. Lloyd-Jones was alive, and he was amused that I told it. He had said that when he was in America some years ago, he was there on one occasion for two weeks. The first week he stayed with friends in White Sulphur Springs, West Virginia—I know exactly where it is. It was a wonderful place where his friends took him and Mrs. Lloyd-Jones. They would take their meals with this couple, and he said there was one thing that began to be a little bit annoying, and that was that this dear man could not finish a meal without criticizing Christians, "so called" as he would put it, who either smoked or drank. Dr. Lloyd-Jones would listen courteously and say, "Well, I can understand how you feel," but the trouble was, he said, the man did it at every meal! After a week they were kind of glad to get away from them—they were always criticizing "so-called Christians." "They call themselves Christians but they smoke and they drink." They couldn't really be Christians, this was the idea.

Lloyd-Jones just said, "*Hmm*—I can see how you feel." They then went from West Virginia to Grand Rapids, Michigan. As soon as Dr Lloyd-Jones told me that, I knew what he was going to say. I happen to know that if you look in a Grand Rapids phone book the names will be mostly Dutch, since a high percentage of the people who live there are Dutch. The story continues: his host picked them up at the airport. The first thing he noticed was that the man who came to meet him at the airport was smoking a cigar! And then, as soon as they got home, he said, "Dr. Lloyd-Jones, would you like a whisky?" They couldn't help but notice the contrast between the two types of Christians over the two weeks. (That is America for you!)

But that is not the end of the story. On the Sunday evening, after the service, as they were driving down the road, Dr.

Lloyd-Jones said, "Oh, look! There is a Howard Johnson's—I love their ice cream. Could we stop and have some ice cream?" And it got quiet. But the man pulled over, went into the parking lot, and Dr, Lloyd-Jones said, "Is everything fine?"

"Sure, fine."

"Are you sure?"

"Fine. Yes."

So they got out, went into the restaurant, and sat—but it was still kind of quiet. Dr. Lloyd-Jones said, "Now look here, I've been with you now for several days—there is something not right. You have gone quiet on me. What is it?"

> We should be grateful for the Christian influence in the West, that we have had Sunday as a special day. There is no command that it has to be a Sunday, however.

"Well, Dr. Lloyd-Jones, this is the Sabbath, and we do not buy ice cream on the Sabbath."

So when they got home, he said to Mrs. Lloyd-Jones, "Everybody has to have something that they are against, it seems."

The spiritual fulfillment of the Sabbath is internal not external. It is what Jesus called "rest for your souls" (Matt. 11:29). It is what God's people are to enjoy as part of their inheritance here below. "There remains, then, a Sabbath-rest for the people of God" (Heb. 4:9). The writer of Hebrews gives a perfect description of what it is like to experience God's rest: "For anyone who enters God's rest also rests from his own work, just as God did from his" (Heb. 4:10). In a word: it is internal.

Should not there be one day in seven set aside for rest and worship? In the perfect world, yes. Sunday has worked very well for centuries. We should be grateful for the Christian influence in the West, that we have had Sunday as a special day. There is no command that it has to be a Sunday, however. No minister gets rest on a Sunday! One day in seven is the biblical hint that we all need a day to rest and not do work.

Sunday became special in church history. But it was only in modern history, that is, after the Reformation, that Sunday was hallowed in a way similar to the way the Sabbath was kept in ancient Israel. There is no biblical basis for this, but when there was an effort to Christianize a nation, they chose the first day of the week to be set aside, and there was nothing wrong at all with choosing Sunday. As a matter of fact, if you go to Saudi Arabia, they keep one day—it is Friday. If you go to Israel they keep one day—it is Saturday. We have a tradition that is rich, and it is based, to some degree, on Christianity. As it could be said, we have it on the books; what a shame to let it slide.

So Sunday is special. And yet there is no evidence that it should be kept in this legalistic way. You couldn't go for a long walk on the Lord's day if you are going to be as the Jews were in ancient times. As a matter of fact, it was to be a day of refreshing. What would be one person's refreshment may not be so for another. The danger is when we become legalistic and give people a guilt trip if they buy an ice cream cone, or if they do anything that would sound like fun. True, that was the way it was in ancient Israel. But that has been done away with. We can keep Sunday special without being legalistic.

Chapter 10

THE FIFTH COMMANDMENT:
THE FIRST COMMANDMENT WITH A PROMISE

Honor your father and your mother, so that you
may live long in the land the LORD your God is
giving you.

—EXODUS 20:12

W E NOW EXAMINE the fifth commandment, which Paul
calls "the first commandment with a promise." He puts
this in the context of family relationships.

Children, obey your parents in the Lord, for this is right.
"Honor your father and mother"—which is the first commandment with a promise—"that it may go well with you
and that you may enjoy long life on the earth."

—EPHESIANS 6:1-3

God might have added a promise to any one of the Ten
Commandments, but He did it only with this one. Why? For
one thing, in ancient Israel this command held the whole nation
together. And today, to the degree this is disregarded, any nation
will crumble. The whole of society hangs together on whether this
command is taken seriously. So, God could have added this word
of promise to any of the commands, but He chose this one, thus

giving an added incentive for keeping this command.

I find this sobering. In the light of this I ask, how long can I expect to live, based on this promise and my attitude toward my own parents? So if this command is true, and the promise is relevant, how long may you expect to live?

You could call this fifth commandment a proposition. God makes a deal with His people. Honor your father and your mother so that you may live long in the land the Lord your God is giving you. We are talking about teaching again. The Ten Commandments tell us the kind of righteousness God wants from those who uphold His name. The Ten Commandments show the minimum righteousness God expects also of those who say they are Christians. So it is teaching, for we all need to be taught.

LEARNING TO KEEP THE COMMAND

Parental respect must be taught. My father used to say to me all the time, especially if I was disrespectful, without apology and without blushing, "Son, the Bible says to honor thy father and thy mother." So I was taught this. Parental respect must be taught in the home and in the church. It is the teaching of gratitude. We need to be taught gratitude, and that means to be thankful and respectful toward our parents. And yet I must admit that this teaching will be easier for some than for others. Not all have good parents. My heart goes out to anybody who struggles here. I was once pastor of a church in which there was a lady who was abused by her father; her father had sexual intercourse with her as far back as she could remember. It messed up her life to no end.

Perhaps you had a father who was cruel and insensitive. Perhaps you had a mother who was not very loving. And now you are told to honor them, and you say, "I can't." I sympathize. I have asked myself in preparing this chapter, can I ask this of everybody? The love for the people I write for is more important than writing. I myself have been so blessed. Just before writing this, as it happens, I have been with my own father. My mother died when I was seventeen; she was only forty-three. My father, aged ninety, is still alive—only just, as he has Alzheimer's disease—and I have asked myself, why am I so thankful for my parents?

126

I can echo the sentiments of David in Psalm 16:6: "The boundary lines have fallen for me in pleasant places; surely I have a delightful inheritance." That also means that I am without excuse. If you too have a father and mother who did not abuse you, but who loved you, did their best for you, and loved the Lord, you ought to be very thankful.

When it comes to this matter of gratitude, we tend to realize much, much later why we should have been so thankful. But God has already shown we should be thankful by saying, "Honor your father and your mother." This means we are to love them equally. You may well have a personal preference as to whom you like more—most of us do, if honest. But what of the person whose father or mother was not very nice? Well, God will not let us be selective here. It is His command; it is His idea. So I come back and ask this question, how long do you expect to live? Based upon this, when taking it literally we can infer: "Honor your father and your mother so that you may live long." Do you expect to live a long time? Do you not have a fairly shrewd idea whether you have honored your father and your mother?

What is the purpose of this command? Why do you suppose God gave it? It is because of the importance of the home. We use the phrase "nuclear family"—husband, wife, father, son, daughter, parents, children. It refers to the family unit.

God loves families. There is something some may not have known: Satan hates families. The anti-God forces at work today are anti-family. As the psalmist put it, "When the foundations are being destroyed, what can the righteous do?" (Ps. 11:3). If children rise up against their parents, everybody suffers. The parents suffer. The children who do it suffer, and oh, how sorry they will be down the road. The nation suffers. So many of the problems that we face at the present time can be traced right back to the family unit. So much begins in the home.

The greatest teaching comes from the home. There is a sense in which you could say that sending children to school to learn what should be taught at home is Plan B. In other words, they are going to learn at school, and so you send them to school and we thank God for schools. I even thank God for the schools I had in Kentucky, although as I look back I can see why one of our slogans for many years was, "Thank God for Arkansas." In Kentucky that was one of our slogans. In the days when there were only forty-eight states, Kentucky was forty-seventh in educational standards; Arkansas was at the bottom!

So I thank God for my schooling. But I wouldn't be where I am if I did not have the greatest dad and the greatest mother in the world. And yet I have asked myself, what exactly did my parents teach me? First of all, they taught me the way of salvation. I learned it in the home, and they took me to church where the gospel was preached, and by the time I was six and a half years of age, I could take it no longer; I said, "I want to be saved." And I knelt at my parents' bedside, on April 5, 1942. I remember it as though it were yesterday. I asked God to forgive me of my sins and come into my heart.

I think of the legacy of my father. What was it? Perhaps I can explain it as it emerged recently. I was in Atlanta, and I sat at lunch around the table with some fairly powerful people. There was John Haggai, who, if I were to guess, could have a legacy greater than Billy Graham's. He has had over 28,000 students so far going through his two institutions in the Far East. His organization brings people out of developing countries—China, the Orient, and what we call the third world—trains them, and sends them back. They are doing what missionaries used to do but largely do not any more. For one thing, in many places missionaries are not welcome. The Haggai Institute pays the students' way to come out, pays their airfare, puts them in school for two weeks, trains them, and sends them back. It is a wonderful thing. I said, "John, what would you say is your greatest gift?" I thought he would say, "Raising money," because I have never seen anyone like him. He has raised money, and he does it by the tens of millions of dollars.

He said, "Picking good friends." Those were his words. I then turned to Dr. Bill Hinson, who is the president of the Haggai Institute, a man of great organizational genius. I said, "Bill, what is your greatest gift?" He said, "Being an encourager." I turned to the man to my right, whose name is Randy Price. I said, "What is your greatest gift?" I thought he would say, "Making money," because he handles assets of $350 million, a young man in his thirties—

a financial genius. He said, "Being trustworthy." And then I turned to the man on my left, who is president of Integrity Music. I said, "What is your greatest gift?" He said, "To get people to experience the presence of God."

Then they turned on me. I should have known that they would. They asked, "What is yours?"

They thought I would probably say, "Preaching the Bible," or "Trying to make people understand the Bible." I said, "Well, I really hesitate to answer you," fearing being misunderstood.

"Come on, we asked."

"All right. But I am doing it to brag on my dad." I said, "A prayer life. I had a dad—he was not a minister, he was not a preacher, he was a layman—who would not dream of going to work without thirty minutes on his knees. That is the way he started the day. And it just rubbed off on me. Spending time alone with God. It is my greatest asset."

My dad also taught me to work. He taught me ambition and motivation. Maybe he gave me too much! I fear I have an overdose of drivenness. He would drive me to mow the lawn or rake leaves. He made me get a job selling a weekly newspaper called *Grit*, which I sold to all the neighbors when I was only ten. When I was twelve I had a daily job of delivering the Ashland, Kentucky, *Daily Independent*. This is not because my family needed the money; my dad did not want me to be lazy. But there is no doubt whatsoever in my mind that I would never have achieved anything, including good marks in school, had I not had him to push me. I now thank God for that, even if Dad was not perfect.

He taught me to tithe. The first week after selling *Grit* we sat at our dining room table and counted up my profit for the week—fifty cents! I was so proud of myself, whereupon Dad put his finger on a nickel (five cents) and pushed it to one side: "That is the Lord's."

I put my finger on that nickel and brought it back with my well-earned money. "That is mine."

"No, son, that is the Lord's." Dad won. I am so glad he did. Tithing must be taught—the sooner, the better.

Dad taught me to keep myself pure. He warned me about the dangers of sex and the importance of waiting for the right person

GRACE

to come into my life. I fear that this sort of thing is very neglected in homes today. The things I resented at the time—hard work, tithing, self-discipline—I now thank God for. It is not hard for me to keep the fifth commandment.

My mother gave me a love for music and culture. She was an accomplished pianist. I learned to play the piano and the oboe. To this day I can get as much inspiration from Rachmaninov, Tchaikovsky, and Grieg as from Charles Wesley and Graham Kendrick! My mother was also a woman of prayer. Just before I left for school each day she would put her hand on my shoulder and pray for me.

For those who struggle in having to honor their parents, I have to say how kind God is to attach this command with a promise—to motivate us.

From both of my parents I learned being affectionate—they hugged me. Some people never hug each other or their children, and one is not better off for it. It is my opinion that children not getting hugged by their parents, even after they get older, are deprived. But unaffectionate parents can't help it; they too are products of their past.

A THREEFOLD PROMISE

Why did God give us the promise in connection with the fifth commandment? To motivate us. If you want to live a long time, honor your parents. We all need motivation, especially if we do not like our parents. God keeps a record of each person's behavior. All of us. And if you have had a bad parent, do you know what I reckon? You get a double blessing. After all, I do not need a lot of grace to love my dad or to respect my parents. But for those who do not have very nice parents, perhaps you get a double blessing if you honor them. It is as if you live with a man who is not a very nice husband but you submit to him. God notices that. So too when one loves a wife even when she is not being very lovable (Eph. 5:22–25).

What does this mean, to honor your parents? It means to respect; to hold in a sense of awe. When you are young, you obey;

when you are old, you honor. You treat your parents with dignity. And by the way, it will come home to you. Some may think being old is so far along the road that it is going to take forever to get old—I will tell you now, it will seem like seconds and you will be old, and you will remember how you were with your dad and mom.

The ultimate practice of this command in any case is always fulfilled by walking in the Spirit. To those who have bad parents, that is the only way you are going to keep this command. By walking in the Spirit. For if you did not have very good parents and you go by the flesh, you are going to hate them and want vengeance on them. But if you walk in the Spirit, that means you will forgive your parents and honor them.

We all have to forgive our parents. I have been bragging about both of my parents in this chapter. But as I said, my dad was not perfect. Neither was my mother. I could spend a lot of time talking about their faults and ways in which they damaged me quite severely. But I have forgiven them, for two reasons: first, I understand in some ways why they were like they were—they couldn't help it; and second, it is my Christian duty to forgive in any case. I could offer a third reason: I want my children to forgive me for my imperfections and consequent damage done to each of them.

When I began my thesis at Oxford in 1973, I will never forget what my supervisor, Dr. Barrie White, said to me early on: "Spend time with your children; you will not get these years back." I did not much, and the years are gone. I spent more time in the Duke Humphrey wing of the Bodleian than anywhere else. I said to myself, "The sooner I get this thesis written, the sooner we'll get back to America, and then I will spend time with them." The next thing I knew I had accepted the pastorate at Westminster Chapel. I rationalized again that it is more important to put God first, and I said that putting the church first (including countless hours of sermon preparation) was the right priority. Wrong. I now believe I would have preached just as well (maybe better) and the church would have done as well (maybe better) had I put the family first.

In a word: I hope my children will forgive me as I have

forgiven my parents for their failures. But I certainly would understand if our children struggle in this area.

Honoring one's parents, after all, is a command. A command from the Lord is issued because it is needed. It is issued because it goes against what we naturally may feel. For those who struggle in having to honor their parents, I have to say how kind God is to attach this command with a promise—to motivate us. To put it bluntly, if you do not want to honor your parents, do you not want to live a long time? Perhaps that promise—God gave it especially to those who need it—will help ensure we do not grieve the Spirit by bitterness and that, as a bonus, we enjoy more years than we would have otherwise.

Remember, then, no parent is perfect, and so yours were not perfect. The only training we get as parents is from our parents who were not perfect. Where do you think your parents got their training? They got their training from their parents, and they were not perfect. And they got their training from their parents, and they were not perfect! This is partly why we are told that the sins of our fathers will be visited upon the children down to the third and fourth generation. We pass it on. We grow up saying, "When I get to be a dad, I am not going to be like my dad." But we are! "I will not be like that when I get old." But we are! It is because we imitate the way we were brought up.

Most parents carry a great sense of guilt over their mistakes, failures, and shortcomings. I will tell you another thing. We do not get a second chance to be a different kind of parent. Once the kids have grown up, that is it; you have had it. You think, *Oh, if I could start all over again, I would do better.* Perhaps. But you do not get a second chance. Neither did our parents.

But most of us get a second chance to honor our parents. You do not get a second chance at being a parent; you do get a second chance to honor your parents. Because if up to now you have not honored them, you can start now. Perhaps you were a disobedient child. But you can be a son or daughter who puts it right years later—by honoring your parents. This is really an encouraging commandment. If our parents are alive, it is not too late.

You may say, "What if my father or mother is dead?" I will tell you what, you can start thanking God for them. Honor them by thanking God for the good they did. Start counting your blessings and tell them to the Lord. He will like that. If they are still alive, begin now to honor them.

My own dad had a very strong personality, and he never saw me as a man but would treat me as if I was a child! I never will forget the first time he came to Westminster Chapel. I died a thousand deaths. He went back into what we used to call the parlor, and he said, "Where's the boy?"

Sir Fred Catherwood came up and said, "Excuse me, Mr. Kendall, can I help you?"

"Where's the boy?"

"Sorry?"

"Where's my son?"

"Oh, you mean Dr. Kendall!"

"Yeah, where's the boy?"

I was so embarrassed. But he meant no harm.

Until a very few years ago that is the way he treated me. He would write and say to me, "I wrote to you on the fourteenth, you had to have had that letter by the eighteenth, you have waited at least three days to answer me." I mean, he would talk to me like that! Two or three times a month. And then the day came when I did not get any more letters. I miss them. They call it "the long good-bye." Alzheimer's.

So, if your mother or father is still alive, and you have not been all you ought to be, do you know what you ought to do? Pick up the phone and say, "I love you."

Once our son TR wrote me a letter, a little note, just before I was to fly from England to America. I took it with me and read it on the plane. I read it nearly every day while away. You know why? At the end he said, "I love you." A mother and father love to hear that from their kids; it means everything.

According to the apostle Paul, the fifth commandment actually has a threefold promise: first, "that it may go well with you" and second, "that you may enjoy long life on the earth" (Eph. 6:3). It is amazing how you can read something a dozen times, one hundred times, five hundred times, and then you see it for the first time! I never noticed that until recently. I knew about the part "that you may live long," but He says "that it may go well with you." Could it be that you aren't prospering in some sense because you have not honored your parents? "That it may go well with you" implies a quality of life now—as well as the promise of long life. But Paul also says in Colossians 3:20 (and this is the third part of the promise): "Children, obey your parents in everything, for this pleases the Lord." You can therefore honor your parents, and it pleases Jesus. Do you want to please Jesus? Honor your parents. That is the third promise inherent in the fifth commandment! The promise is a life that is long, prosperous, and pleasing to the Lord. What's more? You feel good.

ETERNAL LIFE

However, there is a difference between the promise inherent in the fifth commandment and the promise of eternal life. Earthly life comes from honoring your parents. But that in itself will not save you. So you say, "Well, I've honored my parents." It may give you a long life, but it will not save you. Eternal life, though it begins now—the moment you receive Jesus as your Savior—will last forever. "For God so loved the world that he gave his one and only Son, that whoever believes in him shall not perish but have eternal life" (John 3:16). Eternal life begins now and lasts forever. That is by grace. God just gives it to you. But the fifth commandment has some conditions, and complications, as we will see below.

There is a sense, then, in which living a long time is not only by grace, but also by works, because if you honor your parents God promises to give long life. But if you go to heaven it will not be because of honoring your parents or of any other good thing you did. Honoring your parents, I repeat, is something that you ought to do, and it will affect your quality of life here below, but in itself it will not save you. Salvation begins when you recognize that you have sinned and you stop blaming your parents, because there comes a time when you say, "The buck stops here." Some have blamed parents for everything, and the problem is that one needs to stop it and say, "What kind of a person am I? And if I am a parent what am I going to be like?" If you judge your parents, one day you too will be judged, and it could be far worse. It could be that you will deserve far worse than what you think your parent deserves.

What about people who honored their parents but died before old age? David Brainerd, the godly missionary to the American Indians, died at twenty-nine. The saintly Scottish preacher Robert Murray M'Cheyne died at twenty-nine. Spurgeon died at fifty-eight. My mother died when she was forty-three. Why? I do not know. There is a lot I do not know. And I do not have a good answer for all questions put to me. If I knew all the answers I wouldn't need faith. The apparent exceptions I can only leave with a loving, wise God who will give the answers in heaven. There is a reason for all God does and permits. I will not let what appear to be exceptions to this promise deter me from holding fast to God's Word. I do not want to fail in honoring my parents. Do you?

If you have failed in honoring your parents you can still have eternal life. That is the wonderful thing. You may say, "I do not think I am going to live a very long time because I have not been a very good son, I have not been a very good daughter, so I do not deserve to go to heaven." None of us deserves heaven. But God will save those who turn to His Son, and He may also be gracious by giving one a long life.

I will tell you the best news of all: Jesus was the perfect Son. Talk about one who honored His Father! Jesus honored His Father; He was the perfect Son. He also remembered His mother at the cross (John 19:26–27). And the righteousness of Jesus—which includes honoring parents—will be put to your credit the moment you believe. The moment you transfer the trust that you had in your good works to what Jesus did for you on the cross—in that moment you are given a pardon, eternal life. You will go to heaven because the righteousness of Jesus—His being a perfect Son—is put to your credit so that in God's sight you have been a perfect son, a perfect daughter.

You might live a long time, then, but you will not necessarily go to heaven. Suppose you live until you are eighty. I would call that a long time. What if you live until you are ninety, but then lose your soul? So eternal life is far more important than long life here below. "What good is it for a man to gain the whole world, yet forfeit his soul?" (Mark 8:36).

I will make one last point before I close this chapter. Colossians 3:20 says, "Obey your parents in the Lord." That means that you put obedience to Christ first. There was a woman at Westminster Chapel whose father was a Muslim, and she had since become a Christian. She had not dishonored her father; she respected her father. She wrote and phoned him all the time. "Honor your parents in the Lord." You may not agree with them, and they may not be Christians, but you do not have to dishonor them.

Chapter 11

THE SIXTH COMMANDMENT:
THE SIN NOBODY ADMITS TO

You shall not murder.

—EXODUS 20:13

I'VE CHOSEN THE title for this chapter, "The Sin Nobody Admits To," because if someone commits the crime of murder, they are probably going to cover it up. They are going to deny it. They will do anything not to have to pay the penalty. So they will plead not guilty. Or they might plead guilty by reason of insanity. So one is not going to admit to murder.

WHAT IS MURDER?

As the King James Version puts it, "Thou shalt not kill." The Hebrew word means "to murder." It refers to an act of extreme selfishness to remove a threat. It shows that one has no concern for another person's life. When there is a threat, you remove it—whether that threat be from an enemy or an unborn baby. This does not refer to killing animals or vegetation; such is not murder.

Murder has its origin in the human heart. "For out of the heart come evil thoughts, murder, adultery, sexual immorality, theft, false testimony, slander" (Matt. 15:19). It refers to a selfish, sinful heart. One commits murder because he or she hates. It is the result of an obsession—when your thoughts are occupied continually, and you decide to remove this person who is a threat to you. King Saul became obsessed with David; he was more threatened by David than he was by the Philistines—the ancient enemy of Israel—and was driven to remove David (1 Sam. 18).

The sixth commandment, therefore, does not refer to plants, animals, or even war or capital punishment. Why? There is no personal hatred in such cases. Murder is carried out because of hate, when you want to remove a human being who threatens you in some way.

The Law required that the murderer be accountable for his or her sin. One had to face judgment, and if found guilty, the person was to lose his life. That in itself proves that the sixth commandment does not refer to capital punishment, for the punishment for murder was death. There were legal proceedings. There was a court set up in every town that dealt with criminal matters. This was to ensure that a person was given a trial. But if found guilty, the punishment was death.

THE GOSPEL VIEW

This, however, only referred to the physical, external act of murder—killing another because of hatred. But there is another way to look at it if we accept what Jesus says, for in the Sermon on the Mount, we have Jesus' own interpretation of the sixth commandment (Matt. 5:21–26). He went so far as to say that if you get angry you have already committed murder! How many of us are prepared to admit that we have murdered if we get angry? We do not admit to murder; it is the sin nobody admits to. According to Jesus, if you hate, or if you are angry, you have therefore committed the sin of murder; you have broken the sixth commandment.

We do not naturally admit that anger is murder or that hate is murder. We do not admit that holding a grudge is murder. We do not admit that if we do not forgive, and do not forgive totally, it is murder. If we gossip, we do not admit that it is murder. You say,

"Well, how can gossip be that?" It is because gossip, like jealousy, is a part of the family of hate. A person is jealous because he hates, and hate is murder. The first account of murder in the Bible is recorded in the fourth chapter of Genesis, when Cain killed his brother Abel (Gen. 4:1–12). It was all because he was jealous, which stemmed from hate and led to murder.

Not all jealousy and hatred leads to physical murder. We act out our jealousy by thriving on gossip, especially if that gossip centers on making a person look bad. We get jealousy out of our system via gossip. We love to say what makes another look stupid; we want to listen to what makes a person appear less credible. It feels good. We feel entranced. It is all phony, of course, and is never fulfilling. But we tell ourselves this is good to indulge in.

I remember sharing with two ministers a story I heard about a well-known pastor in the area I once lived. I am not proud of it now. But because the story was true I felt no restraint at the time. This pastor was having an affair with his secretary, and the story broke that week. The two ministers hadn't heard about it. "We love it," each said. "Tell us more." I did not know at the time that the pastor who had fallen was a serious threat—a rival—to the two ministers. It was delicious news to them. I too had been jealous of this pastor, and I enjoyed telling it. Sadly, I felt no need to repent of what I did. I have not seen the two ministers since. But as I write these lines, this story has come back to me. I was guilty of not only jealousy and hate but, according to Jesus in Matthew 5:21–22, murder. I grieved the Spirit but did not feel a thing. The sobering truth about grieving the Holy Spirit is that we seldom feel it at the time. I have since repented and pray that I will always refuse to contribute or listen to information that makes my brother or sister look bad. It is judging, moreover, and I am warned (Matt. 7:1–2) that what I have reported about another could happen to me as well.

In the same way that jealousy stems from hate, then so also does gossip stem from jealousy. If we did not have jealousy in us we would not care for gossip. We wouldn't do it; we wouldn't listen to it. It is all a part of the same family: hatred.

We do not admit that hurting another person's reputation is murder. We do not admit that if we want to make another person feel bad, that is murder. We do not admit that if we want another person to suffer, that is murder. We do not admit that if we want to discourage another person, demoralize him, take the wind out of his sails, that Jesus says it is murder. We do not admit that if we abuse verbally, it is murder.

Jesus said, "He that is faithful in that which is least is faithful also in much" (Luke 16:10, KJV). What that means is that if you are faithful in a little bit, in that which is least, even the smallest thing—because that was your only opportunity to show whether you would be faithful—that is a test, and it shows you would also be faithful in much. Take, for example, the great martyrs of centuries before and some martyrs of this generation; read their biographies. Your first reaction may be, "Oh, I do not believe that I would ever have faith like that, that I would die for the Lord." The way to tell whether you would die for the Lord is whether you are faithful in that which is least. If you obey whatever God tells you to do, even the little things, it shows you are prepared and able to be trusted with something big.

I refer to this mainly because Jesus went on in Luke 16:10 to say, "He that is unjust in the least is unjust also in much." That means, if you sin just a little bit by gossiping or by jealousy or by abusing another person verbally, then you would sin also in much; you would do the extreme thing. Given the circumstances, given the situation, you are capable of committing a sin equal to any heinous crime that you have ever read about.

You may say, "I do not agree with that." I can only say this: it is what Jesus said. Furthermore, if you and I were to become totally and transparently honest, and begin to look into our hearts and see what we are capable of, we would have little difficulty believing what Jesus said about it. The more I see of my own heart, I can tell you now, it scares me to death. And I just think, *Lord, it is only by Your grace that I am kept from doing that which would put me in prison.*

Jesus said that if you lose your temper you have committed murder (Matt. 5:22). Have you ever done that? If you make another person feel guilty—are you good at that? Are you good at giving a person a guilt trip? You have committed murder. If you make another person feel that he or she is a failure, and you make a person feel worthless, you have committed murder. If you do not want a person to be successful, you have committed murder. It is a matter of the heart, says Jesus. It is the way God sees us. When I make another person feel guilty because I am angry, it is because I want him or her to feel pain. I want to punish. I say, "You should feel bad about this—I do not think you feel bad enough," so I say what I think will send that person on a real guilt trip. As I said before, guilt is probably the most painful feeling in the world. And when I make another feel guilty, I am being cruel. I would never want to commit physical murder, but I excuse myself if I kill a person's spirit and drive him or her to feeling awful.

God never oppresses us. The devil does. Therefore when I oppress another person by making them feel worthless, I am in that moment not God's instrument but the devil's. The devil is the accuser (Rev. 12:10). The devil was a murderer from the beginning (John 8:44), and I am keeping up what he started by being an accuser of people.

If I say what will keep another from succeeding, I have in that moment violated the sixth commandment, according to Jesus. I cannot bear a rival—or anyone I do not like or who I feel does not deserve to be elevated—being greatly admired. So I say just a small word about him or her: "What do you really know about John?" I then proceed with the rationale, "I am saying this to you for your own good." It is probably true that when a person says, "I am saying this to you for your good," he is up to no good.

The paradox is that the closer we get to God, the more sinful we feel, and the more we see what we are really like. We begin to be convicted of sin that hadn't even begun to bother us up until then. One evidence that true revival has come will be when under the Holy Spirit's anointing we begin to see what we are truly like and feel awful about it. And so when I write like this, it may seem so strange and so extreme to say that wanting to discourage another person is murder. But when we are under the anointing of the Spirit we will be like Isaiah, who, when he saw the glory of the Lord, said, "Woe to me!" (Isa. 6:5). Isaiah had been used by God up until then and was a morally upright person. Were the Holy Spirit to come into our churches in great power you would possibly not think of another person. You would in that moment think of yourself and be conscious of your sin. The Spirit would show us what Jesus told us is true and make each of us see this and our capability.

Jesus had a further purpose in interpreting the sixth commandment as He did. He said, "Anyone who is angry is subject to the judgment." As I said above, the ancient system had courts in every town to deal with an accused murderer. Jesus merely says, "Subject to judgment." He means that the eye of God sees all that we are thinking. Sometimes people do get away with murder. But when it comes to the eye of God—that sees all including what is in the heart—it has a way of stepping in on its own. "You may be sure that your sin will find you out" (Num. 32:23). It may well also refer to God's final judgment when every secret will be revealed. The ancient Law had nothing to say about anger; it only restrained the expression of anger, namely, murder itself. There was no legislation against anger. It only legislated against anger when it showed itself in some visible crime.

But there is more. Jesus said, "Anyone who says to his brother, 'Raca,' is answerable to the Sanhedrin. But anyone who says, 'You fool!' will be in danger of the fire of hell" (Matt. 5:22). *Raca* refers to jealous anger. It is name-calling. *Raca* literally means "empty." It is the equivalent of calling a person empty-headed or stupid. It is insulting another's intelligence. When we are jealous, we usually love to make another person look stupid or unintelligent. We do not admit to jealousy; we merely go on the attack to say things that insult. We make catty, spiteful comments—whatever will put another down.

Probably the oldest trick in the book to make a person look bad is to imply that he is not very bright. It is a convenient way of classifying a person—putting one into perspective—so he will not seem to be so great a threat. I may say something about a rival that implies he is lacking in intelligence, such as, "He only got that position because of whom he knows—he just got a lucky break." I resort to this sort of trickery because, the truth is, I deeply resent that he is being blessed or admired by so many people. *It isn't fair,* I say to myself. So I try to make him look inferior. Questioning his natural intelligence is the quickest way to do it.

To call a person a "fool" is going further: it is to judge another person's heart. The Greek word actually means an outcast, apostate, or rebel. This is worse in God's sight than calling a person empty-headed, because calling a person a fool is playing God. Only God can judge another's heart. You are saying this person deserves to go to hell. As someone put it, the person who tells another he is damned to hell is in danger of hell himself. This is a dangerous thing to do, according to Jesus, for this prerogative belongs to God alone.

> If one has not committed the crime of murder, he or she may feel self-righteous. But the Holy Spirit shows that hate and anger are in the heart. That is what Jesus is after.

We have recently had the privilege of having a young Japanese lady in our church. She said that in her culture there is no word in Japanese for "sin." The nearest you can get to that word, she says, is the word *crime*. To get a Japanese person to see he or she is sinful is hard to explain through language. But this young lady said that what convicted her at the end of the day was seeing how self-righteous she was. That is something only the Holy Spirit can do.

Seeing our own self-righteousness is what Jesus is referring to in the Sermon on the Mount. As I have said earlier in this book, that sermon is part of Jesus' doctrine of the Holy Spirit. If one has not committed the crime of murder, he or she may feel self-righteous. But the Holy Spirit shows that hate and anger are in the heart. That is what Jesus is after. What was most remarkable was that this Japanese lady testified to seeing how sinful it is to be self-righteous.

Seeing the sin of self-righteousness is a hallmark of the work of the Holy Spirit. And the only hope I have of anybody being moved by this chapter is that one becomes convicted of self-righteousness. It is one thing to be convicted that you have lost your temper but another to see it as self-righteousness. Perhaps you are convicted that you have held a grudge—you cannot forgive—and that is good. I want the Holy Spirit to do that. But if anyone is convicted of self-righteousness, it shows that God is powerfully at work. God hates self-righteousness because it always bypasses the death of Jesus on the cross. Self-righteousness always says, "I can make it on my own. I do not need a mediator. I do not need a substitute. I do not need somebody to plead my case; I can make it very well on my own, thank you very much." God hates that.

If you believe that you are good enough to go to heaven, that your righteousness without a mediator will satisfy God's justice, you are not a Christian. I do not care how moral you are, if you have been baptized a thousand times, or if you are an upstanding church member. You may be a deacon or in the clergy. It is only the Holy Spirit who can make us see that we are sinful and that our self-righteousness is sin.

Murder was a crime long before the Law came. Murder is arguably the worst crime there is. But hatred is subject to God's judgment. It means the refusal to forgive; the choice to remain bitter. Forgiving another is a choice we must make—and never look back. Physical murder is a crime as well as a sin; holding a grudge is a crime against the Spirit and therefore sin. It is heinous in God's sight and will rob any of us of an enriched life.

One of the popular views around today is reincarnation. Reincarnation is a delusion of the devil to get you to think that if you do not do too well in this life, in the next life you will have a second chance, and it goes on and on. That is of the devil so that you will not take this present life seriously. You need to know that this life—this side of eternity—is all there is. In other words, the life you have now is the only life you will ever have. The body you have now is the only body you will ever have. That is why you ought to take good care of it. God has given you that body; God has given you that life. The worst thing a person can do is to take another person's life, to deprive that person of the right to live. It is a heinous crime.

Why is it so heinous in God's sight? Murder competes with God. God is against murder because we are made in the image of God (Gen. 1:26–27). Only God can give life, and only God can take it away. Breaking the sixth command, "You shall not murder," is playing God. God said, "It is mine to avenge; I will repay" (Deut. 32:35). If you take vengeance into your hands, you have in that moment become God's competitor.

TRUST IN GOD

When God says, "It is mine to avenge," He means, "Vengeance is what I do best. This is what I love to do and promise to do." God hates injustice. God does not like it if somebody has done something to you that is unfair. If somebody has hurt you, lied about you, abused you, walked all over you, killed your reputation, or stopped you from getting that promotion and you are hurt, God is hurt a lot more than you are. He wants to do something about it. And He will do something about it. He promises to do something about it. That is why He said, "It is mine; I will repay." I say to anybody reading these lines, if you have been hurt, abused, lied about, or your reputation has suffered because somebody was out to get you, it got God's attention—just like that! And God in that moment began to set in motion a way to deal with that person.

What often happens, however, is that we are afraid that God is not going to act soon enough, so we take it into our hands to act instead. And the moment we start to do it, God says, "Oh, you want to do it?" And what you then do is as bad in His sight as what they did to you. Because they committed murder, you are about to commit murder. They destroyed your reputation, so you want to get even. And so God just stays off your case entirely and lets you have a go. And for that reason, sadly, you will never know what God would have done.

It is ironic but true that there is a sense in which the cruellest thing we can do to our enemy is to do absolutely nothing. For that way God Himself rolls up His sleeves and gets involved. He only steps in when we get out of the picture. But if we get into the matter of either vindicating ourselves or punishing another (because God is not working quickly enough), God gets off the case quicker than you can bat an eyelash. But once He can see we are truly out of the picture, God gets into the act. And His vengeance can be devastating. That is why the cruellest thing we can do to our enemy is to do nothing; God does it instead and will carry out justice a thousand times greater than we could have imagined. This was the genius of Mordecai when he did not try to get even with Haman. Mordecai simply let God act—and that is what the Book of Esther is all about. (See Esther 3–7.) I must add, however, that we should pray for our enemies. That does not mean praying that they will be punished, but that they will be blessed. And God may just decide to bless them indeed. But has He not blessed each of us as well—when He could have thrown the book at us?

On the other hand, God may say, "Enough is enough," when it comes to someone damaging us. I can tell you, when He steps in, it is pretty awful. But seldom does God get a chance to do it, because we do not wait for His timing. I believe that quite often He does not do anything right away just to see whether we are going to leave it to Him. He may take a good while to see if you will turn it over to Him, and after a while He says, "Well, now I've been watching so-and-so. It is not good what they did to you. I did not like it then. I do not like it now, and I can see you are not going to defend yourself." One day, a day that will begin like any other day, God will step in.

As I said, the Bible is not against capital punishment, because the same God who said "Do not murder" in Exodus 20 instituted the death penalty in Exodus 21. It is not a word against war because God sometimes led Israel into battle. And there is a clause in the Law for self-defense—sometimes a policeman will defend a person who is just about to get shot, and that would not be regarded as murder. But sometimes God does intervene in such a way that we recognize that He has rolled up His sleeves, and that is the privilege He wants. But it was a biblical principle that punishment should be appropriate to the crime.

The main thing about this command is that it covers the principle of vindication. That means when you want your name cleared, God says, "Leave it to Me." But when you try to discredit another person, you are competing with God and keeping Him from doing what He does best.

It is possible to be angry without it being murder, because the Bible talks about righteous anger. The Bible says, "In your anger do not sin" (Eph. 4:26). This shows that there can be anger that is not murder. Jesus went into the temple and drove out the money-changers (John 2:14). He was angry with sin. But what Jesus was against was hate, the refusal to forgive.

Jesus went on to say in the Sermon on the Mount, "Do not judge, or you too will be judged" (Matt. 7:1). If you judge, you are going to be judged. And so, when He says that if you are angry you are subject to judgment, that means that your anger is an open invitation to God to step in at any moment and judge you. I know. I have had it happen to me. I know what it is to lose my temper and say things out of control. Before I know it I have put my foot in it and look far worse than the person I was judging. In fact I found myself saying things that so betrayed my own self-righteousness that I began to look wicked. If only I had controlled my temper. How right James is: "The tongue also is a fire, a world of evil among the parts of the body. It corrupts the whole person, sets the whole course of his life on fire, and is itself set on fire by hell" (James 3:6). All hell breaks loose once I begin to judge another. It means then and there I have lost control and have broken the sixth commandment. So the next time you begin to lose your temper, remember, in that moment you should be saying, "God, I am right now being subject to judgment; come and judge me." The next time you gossip, or you verbally rejoice at another person's downfall, you are subject to His judgment; you are inviting God right then to come in. The next time you discredit a person, say something that will hurt their reputation, be careful. For if you are angry, you are open to judgment.

James 3:6, quoted above, is a scary description of how not controlling the tongue gives the devil a chance to get in. Our losing control of the tongue gives the devil a right to come straight in, and before you know it, you have said everything under the sun and you think, *What have I done? What have I said?* The devil got in. All hell breaks loose. The judgment of God in this case was giving Satan permission to get into the act.

As we saw earlier, Satan was a murderer from the beginning (John 8:44). Satan brought death to the human race. He knows how to play into our weaknesses. And if this chapter has done nothing more but to show how frail we are, it should make us fall on our faces and say, "God, have mercy on me." For murder is an attitude of the heart. And when we are in a wrong frame of mind, Satan sits on our shoulders and whispers in our ears things that get us even more upset. We begin to have conversations in our minds about the way a person has dealt with us, and the devil will say, "There is more that you have not even thought of. Remember this?" "Oh, yes!" You do not realize that you are getting all riled up and all upset—the fire of hell. Satan gets in.

Walk in the Spirit, and you will not fulfill the hatred of the flesh. You will forgive. You will not be making room for the devil. When we walk in the Spirit, the devil cannot get to us successfully or work through us to hurt others. Walking in the Spirit will mean being more like Jesus.

Chapter 12

THE SEVENTH COMMANDMENT:
THE SIN EVERYBODY TALKS ABOUT

You shall not commit adultery.

—EXODUS 20:14

THE SEVENTH COMMANDMENT is the best-known of the Ten Commandments. I expect, popularly, when people think of the Ten Commandments they immediately think about the seventh one, "Thou shalt not commit adultery," as it is put in the King James Version. Adultery is the sin everybody talks about. It is what sells newspapers, perks up TV ratings, provides fodder for gossip columnists, gives the world its most interest in the church when it touches the clergy, and provides the greatest glee when it threatens to bring down an enemy.

In 1969 there were two major events taking place at the same time. Neil Armstrong walked on the moon, but at the same time Senator Edward Kennedy of Massachusetts was taking a ride in his car with a young lady whose name will long be remembered, Mary Jo Kopechne; they tumbled off the bridge at Chappaquiddick. In the news the next day—wherever you were in the world—there were major headlines: "Man Walks on the Moon" and the event of Chappaquiddick. As a matter of fact, when President Nixon

149

went to the South Pacific personally to welcome Neil Armstrong back to Earth on his return from the moon, aides said that Nixon was far more interested in what happened at Chappaquiddick. He kept an open phone line the whole time to know the latest developments, hoping that his rival, Ted Kennedy, would go down politically because of this sexual scandal.

I remember watching television on one occasion during the late autumn of 1998. Three major world events dominated the news at the same time: first, Saddam Hussein's latest threat in the Gulf; second, the pope's visit to Cuba; and third, the impending impeachment of President Clinton because of his affair with Monica Lewinsky. Watching the live event of the pope flying into Havana, one sensed that the broadcasters were torn over which event to cover. There was Fidel Castro watching the pope stepping out of his jet plane—which was only covered live at the last second. For the latest juicy bit about the president's sex life was also being reported in Washington, and it seemed to transcend the threat of bombs being dropped on Baghdad. The truth is, the public was far more gripped over a sexual affair than the other two events combined.

The politicians in Washington who wanted to impeach President Clinton kept saying, "It's not about sex." That reminds me of what we used to say in the hills of Kentucky: "When a fellow says, 'It's not the money but the principle,' it's the money." I equally suspect that when people say, "It's not about sex," it's about sex.

It is the sin everybody talks about.

Why is this? I suspect there are a couple of reasons. It would be hard to prove, but had there been no Ten Commandments—and no seventh commandment in particular—I doubt there would be as much interest in this matter, even in a post-Christian era. Because we know the Bible says that adultery is sin, therefore there is something about sexual sin that causes people to be more interested, knowing it is wrong according to the Bible. This compounds the interest, strangely enough, just to know that it is wrong.

But it may also have to do with something else. It might be best called "sexual jealousy." There are those who will never have an affair like that, but if they hear of somebody who does and gets caught, it makes it very thrilling for them. They can live vicariously in a way. That is why the television evangelists made the headlines a few years ago. Sexual scandal in the church is probably more interesting than sex in Hollywood, or even politics. The world loves to say that Christians are no different from anyone else, and when there is sexual scandal in the church the headlines will be prominent with that.

Billy Graham said that it seems that the devil gets 75 percent of God's best men through sexual temptation. And one reason that the devil will use this, or seize upon this opportunity, is because the devil wants to discredit the name of God. When King David fell to the sin of adultery and then tried to cover it up, he was caught, not by journalists or by a slip of the tongue, but because he was a man after God's own heart. The Holy Spirit revealed the whole thing to the prophet Nathan. The prophet Nathan said to David, "You did it in secret, but I will do this thing in broad daylight...because by doing this you have made the enemies of the LORD show utter contempt" (2 Sam. 12:12, 14). In other words, the enemies of God do not care about the name of God and want the name of God to be discredited. So the devil will work overtime on that, not to mention the fact that he wants to destroy families, as we will see below.

What is adultery? This has become an interesting topic in America. For there is the legalistic definition, and that would include "sexual intercourse involving at least one married person." But Jesus put forward a higher standard, and this is something that people, I think, forget. There are those who want to bring in the Ten Commandments and make them the ultimate test of righteousness. The truth is, the New Testament generally, and what Jesus taught particularly, raised the standard much, much higher than what you have in the Ten Commandments.

We saw in the last chapter, that whereas murder was punishable by death (since it was a crime—physically taking another's life), Jesus raised the standard and said that if you are angry—if you hate—this is murder. Jesus did the same thing with the subject of adultery. He said in the Sermon on the Mount, "You have heard that it was said, 'Do not commit adultery.' But I tell you that anyone who looks at a woman lustfully has already committed adultery with her in his heart" (Matt. 5:27). So whereas the Old Testament definition would apparently restrict it to sexual intercourse involving at least one married person, Jesus said adultery is any sexual relationship outside of marriage. Furthermore, if you lust in your heart you have already committed adultery.

If one says that Jesus' words refer to adultery not fornication (sex before marriage) or to heterosexual not homosexual sin (man lusting after a woman as opposed to lusting after a person of the same sex), that is to argue with the same casuistry that Jesus condemned in the Pharisees. For they felt themselves free of the sin of adultery if they did not have physical sexual intercourse with another man's wife.

God's Reasons for This Commandment

What is the purpose of the seventh command? There may be someone who says, "Why does God have to spoil the fun? Why make it wrong, something that is so pleasurable, something that is so natural? After all, God made us the way we are." What makes sexuality, sexuality is probably two things: first, it is a biological urge; God made us that way. Second, it is closely connected to self-esteem, where a person wants to be affirmed. If you are sexually attracted to a person, that person feels affirmed, if not flattered.

Why would God step in and say, "Sorry, it is wrong unless you are married"? What kind of God would do this? Surely this is not fair, some will say. If you are not a Christian, one reason may be that you do not want to give up a lifestyle that you know you would have to give up if you became a Christian. Because if you become a Christian, you now are part of the family that does not want the name of God discredited. So you must make a choice whether you want the name of God honored and glorified by your life, or choose your own personal pleasure. By nature you want sexual fulfillment in this world between now and the time you die—you want the most fun you can have. But what makes a Christian, a Christian is that he or she wants the honor of God more.

Why would God go right against the way He made us? Never

forget that sex was not born in Hollywood but at the throne of grace. God made us this way, but He said it is to be within marriage only.

Why? The first reason is the self-esteem of the husband or the wife. Nothing is so affirming as to be chosen by another person to be the one she wants to live with the rest of her life. To think that my wife Louise would choose me! When I saw her at Olivet Nazarene College many years ago, I saw the most beautiful girl on the campus, and I was determined to win her

> When God gave the seventh commandment, He had in mind the sense of self-esteem of the person who is married. It is soul-destroying when either partner is unfaithful, and the damage emotionally is incalculable.

and woo her, and I will tell you, it was not easy. I thought I would never get her! But when I finally did, I felt so affirmed.

When a person chooses to marry you, it is affirming. But nothing is so degrading for a person as when her husband is unfaithful, or his wife is unfaithful. It gives one a personal sense of rejection, and some who experience it never recover. God knows we all need to be affirmed. And if no one else on earth will affirm you, it is good to know that your wife affirms you, that your husband affirms you. You have each other, but when either the husband or the wife breaks the marriage vow, it is degrading; it makes one feel so cheap, so worthless.

So when God gave the seventh commandment, He had in mind the sense of self-esteem of the person who is married. It is soul-destroying when either partner is unfaithful, and the damage emotionally is incalculable.

But there is a second reason, and perhaps this is the main reason: the stability of family life. Stop and think about it. If there were no principles concerning sex, what would the human race be like? If every man was like an animal, like a dog or a cat or any animal, and just did what he wanted to do and forgot the offspring, what would we all be like? If you could interview those who are in prison at this moment and find out what their home life was like, most would have been neglected by a father or a mother. Sometimes they come from broken homes; they have no concept of what it is like to grow up with a stable family background. Imagine compounding this again and again. If there were no law, no principle governing marriage and sex, so that everybody could have sex with whomever he wants to without worrying about the babies who would grow up without a father, the consequences would be disastrous.

Had God not given this commandment in ancient Israel, the nation would have collapsed. It would have meant the disintegration of families. There would have been no possibility of genealogies. Sexual promiscuity would have swept the nation. And yet there are thousands of people today who do not know who their parents are. They grow up with unthinkable insecurity and lack of self-esteem.

JESUS' TEACHING

Jesus' interpretation of the seventh commandment refers to the "spirit" not the "letter" of the law on adultery. "The letter kills, but the Spirit gives life" (2 Cor. 3:6). For life in the Spirit leads to a higher standard than that of the Law. Those who want a legalistic interpretation of the Law—particularly the seventh commandment—can find loopholes. For the Law forbade a relationship between a man and a married woman who was not his wife. It did not actually refer to so much that Christians today consider to be immorality. President Clinton believed he did not commit perjury because of the way he interpreted "sexual relations." He was probably taking a pharisaical view of the Law. A sexual relationship with a single girl was not then a crime like adultery. The penalty for such was that one had to get married. Polygamy or having a concubine was not against the Mosaic Law.

Jesus' teaching is therefore wider and deeper than that of the Law. He is concerned about any woman—single or married, Jew or Gentile—unlike the seventh commandment as originally understood. For the ancient code before Jesus' time was largely designed to protect the family and a married Israelite woman. Therefore Jesus is concerned about the earliest stages of sin, in the signaling of the eyes. The ancient Law did not apply until the deed was done. Jesus starts further back—with the intents of the heart.

God, for our good, gave the seventh commandment. It is for the stability of family life. Our Lord's application proves this, because He goes on and talks about divorce. It is interesting that as soon as Jesus talks about the question of adultery, He brings up the subject of divorce. Why? Because this has to do with the stability of the family. It has to do with the sense of well-being and emotional and psychological adjustment of a child growing up. The one who grows up in a home where there was a faithful mother and faithful father—a stable family—will be better off emotionally and psychologically; he or she is less likely to give in to crime—these are just statistical facts. God knew that.

God knows what is in us; He knows our frame, and He remembers that we are dust. The seventh commandment is for our good. God loves families, Satan hates families, and God gave the seventh command to protect the family. When family life is unstable, so also is the life of the nation. And the damage to children is incalculable when adultery is committed. Therefore as soon as Jesus brought up the subject of adultery and how lusting in your heart means you have committed it already, He went on to say, "It has been said, 'Anyone who divorces his wife must give her a certificate of divorce.' But I tell you that anyone who divorces his wife, except for marital unfaithfulness, causes her to become an adulteress, and anyone who marries the divorced woman commits adultery" (Matt. 5:31–32).

What Jesus did, then, was to give the Law concerning divorce a status that was not given in the Old Testament. It is amazing how there are those who say, "What we need is to bring back the Mosaic Law." If we brought back the Mosaic Law (and I can understand why some might like it), you could divorce your wife if you did not like the way she cooked your food! If you just did not like her, give her a divorce! Done! But Jesus said, "No. In the Old Testament it may have been like that. I tell you that anyone who divorces his wife except for marital unfaithfulness causes her to become an adulteress, and anyone who marries the divorced woman commits adultery." So Jesus gave the standard a higher profile than was even thought about in the Old Testament. In Britain today, when a man divorces a woman, in a majority of the cases he has a woman ready to marry. But when a wife divorces the husband, in most cases there is no one else.

In a word: the seventh command is for our good. All of the Ten Commandments are for our good. Live according to these commands and you will have peace.

> My son, pay attention to my wisdom,
>> listen well to my words of insight,
> that you may maintain discretion
>> and your lips may preserve knowledge.
> For the lips of an adulteress drip honey,
>> and her speech is smoother than oil;
> but in the end she is bitter as gall,
>> sharp as a double-edged sword.
> Her feet go down to death;
>> her steps lead straight to the grave.
> She gives no thought to the way of life;
>> her paths are crooked, but she knows it not.
> —PROVERBS 5:1–6

I daresay there are people who would stand and shout with all their strength, if they were given the opportunity and could get away with it, that their lives have been ruined because of sexual indiscretion. God made us in such a way that it is only when sex is confined to marriage that there can be peace and tranquillity and the sparing of deep, deep trouble and regret.

How can you keep from committing adultery? There may be those who say, "Well, I struggle with this; I have a higher sex drive than other people." That is something the devil will put into a person's mind; this is often the case with the homosexual. He believes that his sex drive is higher. I have researched this rather thoroughly, and I can tell you, that is not so. The homosexual does not have a stronger sex urge than the heterosexual. We have a way of justifying ourselves for what we want to do. Sometimes we will use a theological rationale to cover a moral failure.

Let us say there is a person who sincerely does not want to give in to this sin. If you are like that, then I would say these things. First, recognize the origin of sin, and that is, it comes from the heart. Jesus put it like this:

> Don't you see that whatever enters the mouth goes into the stomach and then out of the body? But the things that come out of the mouth come from the heart, and these make a man "unclean." For out of the heart come evil thoughts, murder, adultery, sexual immorality, theft, false testimony, slander.
>
> —MATTHEW 15:17–19

So you need to remember that it is in the heart.

There are, therefore, stages that lead to adultery, beginning with normal attraction—which is not sin. By "lusting," Jesus did not mean natural attraction. It is normal to notice a person of the opposite sex, especially if we think that person beautiful or handsome. The next stage: temptation. And yet this is not sin. I admit that it is not easy to tell the difference between natural attraction and temptation and at which point normal attraction becomes temptation. But temptation is not sin. "For we do not have a high priest who is unable to sympathize with our weaknesses, but we have one who has been tempted in every way, just as we are—yet was without sin" (Heb. 4:15).

But once temptation reaches the third stage—I would call it obsession (a persistent idea that dominates a person's thoughts), it shows that carnal desire has moved in and taken over. The physical act has not been committed, but this is what Jesus meant by adultery in the heart. In 2 Peter 2:14 we read of those who have "eyes full of adultery, they never stop sinning." And yet there is almost certainly a fourth stage: seduction. This is causing another person to lust. Both Don Carson and Michael Eaton believe that the Greek in Matthew 5:28 should be translated "with the purpose of getting one to lust." And yet here too the physical act has not been committed; you only want the other person to lust after you. With the ancient Law, there is no sin here. But according to Jesus, to cause another to lust—the attempt of one to get another obsessed with him or her—is adultery already in the heart.

One of the proofs of the Bible is what it says about sin. You will not find it in philosophy. You will not find it in psychology. You will not find it in architecture, in history. It is in the Bible alone that you get the explanation for the way man is. Consider again: 1969. Every newspaper in the world had two big articles: man on the moon and Chappaquiddick. Here was the greatest achievement in the history of the world from a technological point of view, and yet man in a sexual scandal. We have not improved. The proof of sin is the proof of the Bible. Nothing destroys happiness like sexual sin, but does that stop us? No, we will carry on and inevitably try to make ourselves the one exception to the rule. If one says, "As I have already lusted, I might as well go ahead and do it physically since I have already committed adultery," I answer: Don't be a fool. The actual sin is a thousand times worse and brings incalculable grief.

AVOIDING ADULTERY

If you really want to avoid the sin of adultery, avoid the temptation that leads to that sin. This is also why Jesus went on to say:

> You have heard that it was said, "Do not commit adultery." But I tell you that anyone who looks at a woman lustfully has already committed adultery with her in his heart. If your right eye causes you to sin, gouge it out and throw it away. It is better for you to lose one part of your body than for your whole body to be thrown into hell. And if your right hand causes you to sin, cut it off and throw it away. It is better for you to lose one part of your body than for your whole body to go into hell.
>
> —MATTHEW 5:27–30

What is it that you let yourself do that you know will make it easier for you to slip into sexual sin? What do you read? What do you watch? What kind of magazines do you buy? What kind of company do you keep? Billy Sunday used to say, "The reason people fall into sin is because they treat temptation like strawberry shortcake rather than a rattlesnake." If you really want to avoid sexual sin, you will avoid a situation that would lead you to give in to it. When you willfully go where you know you will be tempted, you are asking for trouble. James says:

When tempted, no one should say, "God is tempting me." For God cannot be tempted by evil, nor does he tempt anyone; but each one is tempted when, by his own evil desire, he is dragged away and enticed. Then, after desire has conceived, it gives birth to sin; and sin, when it is full-grown, gives birth to death.

—JAMES 1:13–15

When Jesus spoke as He did about gouging your eye out or cutting your hand off, He meant it metaphorically; I think most people would know that. But sadly not all have understood that Jesus did not intend it to be taken literally. He was using the hand or eye as an illustration that we must give up what is important to us in order to have peace and enjoy God's blessing. In other words, it is more important to enjoy eternal life than to enjoy temporal pleasure that leads to destruction. But I do know of one case in Chattanooga, Tennessee, where a very simple person literally took a saw and cut his hand off, and they rushed him to the hospital but it was too late. There was just a stub there, because he wanted to follow this Scripture literally. Origen (third century A.D.), one of the church fathers, had himself castrated but later regretted it.

Why did Jesus say that if anyone wants to avoid this, the way to do it is to lose one part of the body rather than the whole body being thrown into hell? It means that you sacrifice what is precious in order to put a curb on what is severely tempting. So that, if there was a person who did not want to come to Christ because he did not want to give up his lifestyle, he would need to ask which is more important: to give up the lifestyle and go to heaven, or to give in to sexual temptation, which will last for a season, and then lose his soul. Is it worth it? Jesus asked the question, pointing to the worst possible scenario: "What good is it for a man to gain the whole world, yet forfeit his soul?" (Mark 8:36). Failure to cut off your hand or gouge out your eye, metaphorically speaking, is to leave yourself vulnerable to temptation that will result in sin that is punishable by the fire of hell.

The New Testament prevention for avoidance of sexual sin is in Galatians 5:16: "So I say, live by the Spirit, and you will not gratify the desires of the sinful nature." Because if you live by the

Spirit, you will not willfully lust. If you live by the Spirit, you will be spared the heinous sin. Listen again:

> My son, keep your father's commands
>> and do not forsake your mother's teaching.
> Bind them upon your heart for ever;
>> fasten them around your neck.
> When you walk, they will guide you;
>> when you sleep, they will watch over you;
>> when you awake, they will speak to you.
> For these commands are a lamp,
>> this teaching is a light,
> and the corrections of discipline
>> are the way to life,
> keeping you from the immoral woman,
>> from the smooth tongue of the wayward wife.
> Do not lust in your heart after her beauty or
>> let her captivate you with her eyes,
> for the prostitute reduces you to a loaf of bread,
>> and the adulteress preys upon your very life.
>> —PROVERBS 6:20–26

Are you involved in an affair at this moment? Stop it! Break it off! Whatever has happened up until now—stop and see what God will do from this moment. "If we confess our sins, he is faithful and just and will forgive us our sins and purify us from all unrighteousness" (1 John 1:9).

PUNISHMENT

What is the punishment of the sin of adultery? In the Old Testament it was equal to the punishment for murder. There were at least two offenses punishable by death: murder and adultery. That lets you know how seriously God takes this matter. So you can learn from the Law; it is a hint as to the seriousness of the sin. In Leviticus 20:10 we read these words: "If a man commits adultery with another man's wife—with the wife of his neighbor—both the adulterer and the adulteress must be put to death." In Deuteronomy

22:22: "If a man is found sleeping with another man's wife, both the man who slept with her and the woman must die. You must purge the evil from Israel." Because in the Old Testament it was physical death for committing adultery, Jesus brought the eternal dimension into it and talked about hell. Even in this life God may bring judgment. Paul said:

> It is God's will that you should be sanctified: that you should avoid sexual immorality; that each of you should learn to control his own body in a way that is holy and honorable, not in passionate lust like the heathen, who do not know God; and that in this matter no one should wrong his brother or take advantage of him. The LORD will punish men for all such sins, as we have already told you and warned you. For God did not call us to be impure, but to live a holy life. Therefore, he who rejects this instruction does not reject man but God, who gives you his Holy Spirit.
>
> —1 THESSALONIANS 4:3–8

There are four ways God punishes this sin.

1. You get caught in this life.
2. You are found out at the judgment seat of Christ (2 Cor. 5:10).
3. God lets you get away with it until He sends you to hell.
4. He punished sin by punishing Jesus (2 Cor. 5:21; Isa. 53:6).

God's ultimate way of punishing sin is by putting on His Son all our iniquity. God charged Jesus with our sexual sin. Jesus took our sin as though He were guilty. He who knew no sin, though tempted like us but without sin, became the object of God's wrath on the cross. This means that all our infidelity and immorality has been paid for by Christ's own blood.

Consider the effect this sin has—in three areas. First, on others. If we have stirred up another to the point of mental seduction, it has hurt that person. If that person is married, you have diverted his or her affection to you—and hurt another's marriage. Second, consider its effect on you. You will have grieved the Holy Spirit and, if you carried it out to the physical act, will have to live with the guilt and shame for the rest of your life. Third, consider how it affects God. He is grieved and dishonored, especially when you go all the way by the physical act. Remember this: "Marriage should be honored by all, and the marriage bed kept pure, for God will judge the adulterer and all the sexually immoral" (Heb. 13:4).

God wants His people to be a holy people. The fact that, in God's sight, adultery and murder have the same punishment shows how serious it is. King David, who was a man after God's own heart, paid severely. Oftentimes, sin will lead to more sin, and there is no sin like sexual sin to lead to a cover-up, and the cover-up is eventually what brought down David. When the prophet went to him and exposed his sin, he said to David, "The sword will not leave your house." This was punishment in this life.

FORGIVENESS

I've not written this chapter to make anybody feel guilty or feel bad. Somerset Maugham put it like this: "There is not a human being alive who wouldn't die of embarrassment if every detail of his private life was held up for public examination."

The Bible says, "All have sinned and fall short of the glory of God." But what about pardon for the sin of adultery? The first thing that you should know is that David was forgiven. David received good news: "The Lord has put away your sin." And Jesus said, "Every sin and blasphemy will be forgiven men; but the blasphemy against the Spirit will not be forgiven" (Matt. 12:31). Adultery is not the sin of blasphemy against the Holy Spirit. Blasphemy against the Holy Spirit is when you deny that Jesus is come in the flesh. The Holy Spirit reveals this truth, but if you go against that truth and deny that Jesus is God in the flesh—that blasphemes the Holy Spirit because it cuts against His essential work, which is to reveal who Jesus is (Mark 3:28-30). Anybody who sees that they have committed the blasphemy against the Holy Spirit, but can confess—and mean it—that Jesus is God, is saved. You have not committed the unpardonable sin if you can confess with your mouth that Jesus is Lord and believe in your heart that God raised Jesus from the dead (Rom. 10:9). The sin of adultery, then, is not the unpardonable sin. God forgives sin. Jesus was much, much harder on the Pharisees with their legalism and self-righteousness than He was with those who had fallen into sexual sin. The Pharisees brought to Jesus a woman taken in adultery and put Jesus on the spot, saying, "Teacher, this woman right here has been caught in the act of adultery. You know what the Law says! What do You say?" They were using this as a trap in order to have a basis for accusing Him. Jesus bent down and started to write on the ground with His finger, and when they kept on questioning Him He stood up and said, "Look here. If any one of you is without sin, let him be the first to throw a stone at her." Then He stooped down and wrote on the ground again.

We will not know until we get to heaven what Jesus wrote on the ground. Some speculate that He might have been doodling, or that He might have been writing the names of certain women with whom those men had affairs. But He just said, "He that is without sin among you, let him cast the first stone." And they dropped their stones and tiptoed away. Then Jesus said to the woman, "Where are your accusers? Where are they? Has no one condemned you?"

"No one," she said.

And Jesus said, "Neither do I condemn you. Go now, and leave your life of sin." (See John 8:3–11.)

Jesus was so sympathetic with this sin. God knows our frame; "he remembers that we are dust" (Ps. 103:14). It is so encouraging to know that. He is sympathetic. And God does not approach you to give you a guilt trip. He is saying to all of us, "There is forgiveness for you."

There is therefore something that God hates more than adultery: self-righteousness. Jesus put it like this in Luke 18. He described two men who went into the temple to pray: one a Pharisee and the other a tax collector.

The Pharisee stood up and prayed about himself: "God, I thank you that I am not like other men—robbers, evil-doers, adulterers—or even like this tax collector. I fast twice a week and give a tenth of all I get." But the tax collector stood at a distance. He would not even look up to heaven, but beat his breast and said, "God, have mercy on me, a sinner."

—LUKE 18:11–13

The words in the Greek, "God, have mercy on me," point directly to the mercy seat in the Old Testament, where the blood was sprinkled that satisfied the justice of God. Literally, he says, "God, be propitious to me." In other words, "Look upon me and have mercy as You look on the mercy seat." God will do that for us.

I do not care how many times you have sinned. You may be a prostitute. You may be a person who has been unfaithful. You may have given into a lifestyle of continual sexual sin, but you can ask God for mercy. He will forgive you. Others may condemn you; the church may condemn you, but Jesus says, "I do not. Go now, and leave your life of sin."

Chapter 13

THE EIGHTH COMMANDMENT: THE SIN WE EASILY JUSTIFY

You shall not steal.

—EXODUS 20:15

WHY IS IT we can so easily justify stealing? Before I deal with the subject of stealing, I want to give an example of how quickly and easily we do it, with either man or God.

The Pharisees wanted to trap Jesus in His words. Keeping a close watch on Him, they sent spies who pretended to be honest. They hoped to catch Jesus in something He said so that they might hand Him over to the power and authority of the governor. So the spies questioned Him:

> "Teacher, we know that you speak and teach what is right, and that you do not show partiality but teach the way of God in accordance with the truth. Is it right for us to pay taxes to Caesar or not?" He saw through their duplicity and said to them, "Show me a denarius. Whose portrait and inscription are on it?" "Caesar's," they replied. He said

to them, "Then give to Caesar what is Caesar's, and to God
what is God's."

—LUKE 20:21–25

These are words from Jesus: "Give to Caesar what is Caesar's."
That refers to the state. And we will avoid paying taxes to the state
any way we can and will look for every loophole and try, if we think
we can get away with it, not to give to Caesar what is Caesar's.

And yet there is more: "And give to God what is God's." God
said that the tithe is His. The tithe "belongs to the LORD" (Lev.
27:30). So if we can avoid it, we will do it every time; we will look
for any loophole, any way that we can justify not having to tithe.

So, if we do not pay our income tax or do not pay our tithe,
we justify it. We justify it one way or the other. We say, "The laws
are unfair," "I do not believe in the present government," "I do not
like the way this nation is run," or "I do not like the way the taxes
are spent." We justify any way we can to avoid paying what the law
says we should.

I know people who, in order not to pay their tithe, will actually
come up with theological arguments against it. I've read them. It
is amazing. Why do you suppose they come up with them? I know
that it is not in pursuit of the truth; they want to avoid tithing if
they do not have to. If I may quote this again: "When a fellow says,
'It's not the money but the principle,' it's the money."

Stealing is the sin we easily justify. It seems that when it
comes to the state, we say, "It does not deserve it," and when it
comes to God we say, "He does not need it; He does not care." One
time somebody stole from the collection bag at our church as it
went by. You think, *In church? How could anybody do that?* Well,
it is because they say, "This church does not need it. I need it more
than this church does."

The sin we easily justify is also a sin we tend to think we will
get away with. Stealing. All stealing is done in such a way that we
do not want anybody to see us. That person who took money out
of the collection bag—he looked both ways and probably had a
slick way of doing it; he has probably done it before. Those who go
in to rob a bank will wear a mask. The thief comes in the night.
We do not advertise if we steal; we do not want anybody to know.

If you take something home from the office that is not yours—whether it is a pencil or pen or paper or some little machine in the office—you say, "Well, they have all kinds of money, and I am not getting what I deserve," and you justify it. Or if you do not give a full day's work, and you clock in a time and report that you have done all your work and you know you haven't, you say, "Well, I deserve what I am getting, and they are not paying me enough." It does not seem to bother us when we do that.

In the days of the old Soviet Union, when godless communism was in full sway and Christians were persecuted, there was actually a change in the attitude of some in Soviet government and management toward Christians. They wanted to hire Christians because they knew that Christians did not steal, and Christians gave an honest day's work. That was happening in the old Soviet Union. So it was an opportunity to show that a Christian was one who was conscientious, who did not steal, who gave an honest day's work—it was a great testimony to the faith.

This commandment is God's idea. He also promised to supply our needs. He said through Paul, "My God will meet all your needs according to his glorious riches in Christ Jesus" (Phil. 4:19). It does not follow that one person will drive a Jaguar because another one does, or that all have the same incomes or the same possessions. But God knows what our need is, and He also knows our wishes. He does not promise to supply the wish, but He promises to supply the need. Because of this, He does not like it if we steal to get things, because He says, "I will give you what you ought to have." If you steal, that means you are not happy with what He's given you. And you want to upstage Him. And you think you can do one better. God does not like it. He wants us to come to our possessions by lawful means, namely hard work, not stealing. "He who has been stealing must steal no longer, but must work, doing something useful with his own hands, that he may have something to share with those in need" (Eph. 4:28).

FIVE REASONS

This eighth command was given for at least five reasons. The first reason is for the protection of our own material possessions. Are you not glad that there are laws about stealing? Have you ever been burglarized? Do you know what that is like?

I can never forget one evening when I came into our home, back in Ashland, Kentucky, and I saw that the curtain was underneath the shut window, and I thought, "That is odd." But I did not think anything further about it. Then, about three days later, my dad said, "You know I have not been able to find—" and named several things. We began to look, and, sure enough, somebody had stolen all kinds of things from our house. They traced the fact that the thief came in on the roof and into my own bedroom, opening the unlocked window (in those days you did not bother to do things like lock a window on the first floor). When he went out he pulled the curtain with him, closing the window so that the curtain was underneath. That is how we knew that was the way he got into the house. It was the most awful feeling. Furthermore, that thief was never caught.

If you have come home and found that somebody has taken what was yours, apart from its value or the sentimental value that you put on it, you have an awful feeling. And you are glad that there are laws against this. God likewise gave us this command for the protection of our material possessions.

The word *stealing* means "to take another person's property without the right or the permission." In other words, to take dishonestly. In order to safeguard what is ours, God gave the eighth commandment.

The second reason is to put a fear in us. It was designed to make us afraid to take what is not ours, because with every law in the Old Testament there was punishment. In the Old Testament God gave the punishment according to the seriousness of the offense. God established certain punishments to warn people of the consequence of stealing. For example, in Exodus 22:1: "If a man steals an ox or a sheep and slaughters it or sells it, he must pay back five head of cattle for the ox and four sheep for the sheep." So if you stole, in the Old Testament you did not simply have to return the item; you had to return many times over the value.

Under Islam they could cut off your hand for stealing. That is a pretty good deterrent. The Mosaic Law is not that strong, but it is nonetheless given so that you will have a fear of breaking it.

The third reason for the eighth commandment is that it teaches us to be content with the possessions we have, which were obtained by legitimate means. The Bible tells us—and it is the result of the fall of man in the Garden of Eden—we are to work by the sweat of the brow (Gen. 3:19). But what we work for and rightfully earn is also rightfully ours to keep. However, God wants us to learn to be content with what we have.

The fourth reason is that we will trust God to supply our need. Some make more money than others, and some have more than others. But this commandment is to teach us so that we will trust God to give us what He wants us to have and take no more. Are you content with what God says you need? Or will greed get in so that you say, "I do not think God is being good enough to me"?

We therefore need to learn to accept the anointing God has given us, which partly means the gift we have: what we can do easily. For some, your anointing means you will make $50,000 a year. For others, your anointing only enables you to have a job that will make you $12,000 or $15,000 a year. Perhaps you do not like it that you do not have an anointing that will enable you to make big money. But God knows you; He knows me. And we must learn to trust Him to give us what He knows we need.

This life is not all there is. Here in this life some have more than others; some have much more than others. But when we get to heaven, we will have everything; we will have it all. God will wipe away all tears. I will be living in a mansion; you will be living in a mansion. There will be no greed, no jealousy. I happen to believe that our reward at the judgment seat of Christ (2 Cor. 5:10) will be determined partly by whether we had accepted the anointing God gave us.

The fifth reason I believe that God has given us the eighth command is that we might develop a conscience by the Holy Spirit. A way that you can know you will keep the eighth command is that you walk in the Spirit. For the moment you become a Christian you are given the Holy Spirit. And we are told to "keep in step with the Spirit" (Gal. 5:25). What that means is that if you listen to the Holy Spirit and do what He says, then God will actually speak to you. You will keep these commands that I've written about. You will never steal when you walk in the Spirit, because when you walk in the Spirit you develop a conscience that makes you sensitive to grieving the Holy Spirit. So you sense what grieves Him. And if you steal, you grieve the Spirit. What happens when you grieve the Spirit? You lose presence of mind. You lose that sensitivity to know God's will.

WALKING WITH GOD

One of the most precious things in the world is communication with God. This means that prayer is a two-way communication. I talk to God, and He talks to me. I talk to Him as though He were right there—literally close enough to touch. David says, "I have set the LORD always before me. Because he is at my right hand, I will not be shaken." (Ps. 16:8). Why did David "set" the Lord before himself? He disciplined himself to recognize God's real presence. David was not making it up, because the Lord really was at his right hand! But in order to concentrate and make sense of talking to God, he "set"—positioned—the Lord before himself in his mind. Because the Lord was indeed there at his right hand. And when we begin to talk to God with this awareness, something follows: He talks with us. Not that we hear an audible voice or see an open vision. But because of our love and knowledge of His Word, and knowing that God is not going to say anything that contradicts His written Word (the Bible), we can sense clearly His speaking with us. It may be a sense of approval. It may be a warning. It may be inner peace. But it is real. We sense a smiling face. I do not want to go one hour without a conscious awareness of God's smiling face. I want to keep a short account. If I make the unguarded comment that might grieve the Spirit, either by saying something unflattering about a person or by speaking sharply to my wife or to my children, I want to know if I grieve the Spirit. I therefore walk in the Spirit, and I learn what pleases Him.

Stealing displeases Him. If I steal I am going to lose presence of mind, that wonderful feeling of being "on top of things," when you can just sense that the anointing is on you. It is not worth losing.

We may not always know we are being tested or watched by someone. John, a friend of mine, took a job working for a judge.

The judge had put a lot of cash under a book on John's desk only a few days after he began work there. The cash was spotted. John, fearing someone else would see it and would steal it, took the cash and put it discreetly in a drawer. Several hours later the judge came in, removed the book, and noted that the cash was not there. He immediately began to accuse John and was about to give him the sack, when John pulled back the drawer to show the judge what he felt was wise to do. The judge was actually pleased. Whether or not that was a fair thing for the judge to do, what is absolutely true is that God sees all. If we develop a conscientiousness about stealing that is sensitive to God's presence, we will not only please Him but also be spared much grief.

We therefore dare not steal, not even a penny. Why? God knows. Every Christian should develop such a sensitivity to the Spirit on all these commands, because they reflect the kind of righteousness God wants for His people.

There is one thing fairly obvious about the eighth command that must not be forgotten: God affirms private ownership of material things. He is not against our accumulating possessions; He's not against wealth. God affirms private ownership.

I referred to communism above. It has proved to be a disastrous kind of economy. It will not work. Some still want as little private ownership as possible and as much government as possible. I do not want to be political, but I must say this: private ownership is not condemned by Scripture. Peter said to Ananias, who had lied about what he had just given to the church, "Did not it belong to you before it was sold? And after it was sold, was not the money at your disposal?" (Acts 5:4). That is proof that it is all right to own. Ananias did not even have to sell the property; it was his. And then when he did sell it, he did not have to give the money away. Ananias's mistake was to lie about giving. God affirms the accumulation of wealth. But many of us—I include myself—probably cannot be trusted with much wealth.

> If we develop a conscientiousness about stealing that is sensitive to God's presence, we will not only please Him but also be spared much grief.

I decided years ago, for reasons that I can't explain, that God is not going to let me be a rich man. I will have to be honest: it hurts a little bit when I see that there are even ministers of the gospel who, apparently, are allowed to make a lot of money. I was also envious when a man once came into the vestry at Westminster Chapel whom I hadn't seen since college days. He was a fellow student with me, the exact same age as myself. I do not know this for sure, but I had reason to believe he was worth $100 million. The same age as me, the same college—and I think, *Lord, thanks a lot!* I do not know whether that man tithes, whether he gives it to God, or what he does, but he is just one example. I could go down a list of one after another. I have even known of ministers who were allowed to make money on the side such as a tourist business or owning hundreds of heads of cattle, and they make a lot of money. I envied them. But years ago God slapped my wrist and said, "No!" I am not allowed to do that.

But I repeat: this world is not all there is. And it is a test of my consecration, to affirm another person who can make and accumulate money and become wealthy. I must affirm him and affirm God for blessing him—and not want to steal or be jealous of him either!

FOUR WAYS OF STEALING

There are four ways we can steal. First, by dishonest gain. What is honest gain? Hard work and living within your income. Living within your income means avoiding going into debt if at all possible. When it comes to debt, I've made every mistake that can be made. I know what it is to go deep into debt and pay for the consequences of it. God dealt with me severely. I think one of the reasons He will not let me make much or accumulate a lot is because of what years ago I saw I would be like. Hard work and living within your income—that is honest gain.

Dishonest gain is getting what you want by unlawful means, namely, stealing. Whether this is stealing another person's money or property, or shoplifting; whether it is clothing, something electronic, or groceries. There was a retired bishop who said he did not blame people for stealing from supermarkets—that was an awful thing to say, encouraging that kind of thing. That man should not be in the ministry; it is a disgrace. God says, "You will not steal." A Christian shouldn't think of doing it.

A second way you can steal is by taking advantage of someone in business. You can use deceit or your intelligence to walk over another person. For example, there is the unscrupulous businessman or lawyer who knows what he is doing and takes advantage of another person. It all may be legal, but God knows.

Without the Holy Spirit, any sin is easily justified. Without the Holy Spirit, stealing is the sin we most easily justify. But with the Holy Spirit, we develop an acute tender conscience. Less money, maybe. But greater peace. And you cannot buy that peace. If you say, "I have to have a little more," you will lose peace. Years down the road you will look back and say, "It just was not worth it."

The third way we steal is by robbing God. "Will a man rob God? Yet you rob me. But you ask, 'How do we rob you?' In tithes and offerings" (Mal. 3:8).

Have you ever wondered how you could rob God? This is a way we steal, and this is the sin we easily justify. The way we rob God is not to give Him what He said was His. What is His? "A tithe of everything from the land, whether grain from the soil or fruit from the trees, belongs to the Lord; it is holy to the Lord" (Lev. 27:30). That means that God puts us on our honor to give Him what is His. Some have robbed God over the years, and they say, "God does not care." He not only cares, but He also keeps records. There is only one way that you can get away with robbing God in this life, and that is if you are not saved. Because if you are not saved, then God has not said that you must tithe because you are not a part of the family; He will deal with you at the judgment instead. "Man is destined to die once, and after that to face judgment" (Heb. 9:27). But if you are a Christian and you have robbed God, almost certainly it is only a matter of time until you will sense His displeasure. And you have wondered why you just can't seem to make ends meet, why you can't seem to pay your bills? You wonder where the money goes? If you rob God, He probably will not let you prosper.

There was a particular church where the pastor was asked by a friend, "How many members are in your church?"

And the reply was, "A hundred and fifty."

"How many of your members tithe?"

He said, "A hundred and fifty."

"What? A hundred and fifty members and a hundred and fifty tithers? That is wonderful!"

He said, "Oh, let me explain. About a third of them give it to God, and God takes it from the rest."

God will get it. One of my deacons back in Fort Lauderdale used to say, "If you do not tithe, God will take it one way or the other." He may not get it for the apple of His eye, the church. But He will not let us get away with it.

There is a verse in Lamentations 3:39 that has gripped me for years: "Why should any living man complain when punished for his sins?" What that means is that if God deals with you now, that strongly indicates that you are saved. Be glad He's dealing with you—a living person being dealt with. God does not deal with the non-Christian; He waits until the judgment. If you are not saved, then you face it. But God will deal with the Christian who robs Him. The most foolish assumption is to say, "God does not see; God does not care."

An important cause of these ways of stealing is simply giving in to greed. "Godliness with contentment is great gain" (1 Tim. 6:6). Paul meant that if you walk in the light, you please the Lord. You will have no bitterness toward anybody, you will try to please God in every way, and you live within your income. Godliness with contentment is great gain. But if we are trying to keep up with the Joneses, or go into debt for something we do not need to impress somebody we do not like, we are in bondage. If we have to have clothes that have a label on them so people will be impressed, we are in bondage. It is so silly, so stupid. But I've done it all.

Paul said:

> We brought nothing into this world, and we can take nothing out of it. But if we have food and clothing we will be content with that. People who want to get rich fall into temptation and a trap and into many foolish and harmful desires that plunge men into ruin and destruction. For the love of money is a root of all kinds of evil. Some people,

eager for money, have wandered from the faith and pierced themselves with many griefs.

—1 TIMOTHY 6:7–10

Many, because of the desire for material things, have lost their faith. Some have lost their anointing. They said, of material possessions, "I had to have it." We do not have to have it. Paul goes on to say, "But you, man of God, flee from all this, and pursue righteousness, godliness, faith, love, endurance and gentleness." These are the things that matter. In Romans 1:28 Paul put greed right next to the most grave of sins. He talked about those who were given over to a mind devoid of judgment. He says that when that happens, they are filled with every kind of wickedness, evil, greed, and depravity. He puts it alongside envy, murder, strife, God-hating, and disobedience to parents. If God gives one up to a mind devoid of judgment, the result is no restraint on the heart. One gives in to greed, and this greed is deadly. "A greedy man brings trouble to his family, but he who hates bribes will live" (Prov. 15:27). If greed is not nipped in the bud, it will destroy.

The fourth way we steal is by dishonoring the gospel. If one does not accept the fact that the only way we go to heaven is because of what Jesus did, by which He gets all the glory, we dishonor the gospel.

When I was pastor at Westminster Chapel, I would talk to people every Saturday on the steps of the chapel during our Pilot Light ministry. I have said to hundreds: "If you stood before God, and He said to you, 'Why should I let you into My heaven?' what would you say?" A typical answer every week goes something like this: "I've been a very good person, and I know God would let me in."

I reply, "I believe that you have been a very good person. But you are wrong, for God wouldn't let you in."

"Oh," they say, "but I believe He would let me in."

I stick to my guns: "No. You see, you are bypassing God's own way we get to heaven."

God designed our going to heaven in such a way that all the glory would go to His Son. And if we try to get to heaven in a way that bypasses what God's Son did on the cross, we are stealing from Jesus the honor due Him. Thus we steal and dishonor the gospel. Because God has determined that those who get to heaven are those who know they have no right to be there.

I met the former prime minister of England, Margaret Thatcher, some years ago, and I had time alone with her, even had my picture taken with her. It turns out that there was a group of men waiting to meet her: the vice president of the United States, the chief justice of the U.S. Supreme Court, the American ambassador to St. James's Court, and several other prominent, high-level people from America. I felt it was such an honor. I did not know why they did not have time with her, but all they got to do was to shake her hand. Then they assembled for a group photograph with Margaret Thatcher. So I tiptoed away. But they said, "Oh, Dr. Kendall, come in!"

I said, "Me?" So I stood there in the front row, and as they got ready to take it, they said, "Smile!" I never felt like such a hypocrite in my life. I did not deserve to be in that picture. But I was invited, and I accepted the invitation. I smiled as if I was supposed to be there.

One day, I am going to be in heaven. And I will think, *This is not right. I am such a sinner. I've fallen short of the glory of God. I've broken this very command that I've written about.* The Bible says, "All have sinned and fall short of the glory of God." God says, "I will give you a home in heaven if you will admit it is not your good works, your church membership, the fact that you were baptized, and not you doing your best. In this way all the glory goes to Jesus and His dying on the cross." It makes me feel utterly unworthy.

That is how I am going to go to heaven. I do not deserve to be there except for one thing: I was invited. I accepted the invitation.

What about you? You are invited.

.

Chapter 14

THE NINTH COMMANDMENT:
THE SIN THAT HURTS US MOST

You shall not give false testimony against your
neighbor.

—EXODUS 20:16

WE LOOK AT the ninth commandment, the sin that hurts us most. By that I mean two things. The first is that when people lie about us, it can do irreparable damage. When people lie about us, we are at the mercy of those who believe what they heard, and sadly people too often tend to believe what they hear. So we are dealing with a sin that can hurt us very deeply indeed.

But there is a second thing I mean by this being the sin that hurts us most, namely, how we ourselves are hurt when we do not tell the truth. For example, it will cause us to develop an insensitive conscience. The Bible talks about having a conscience "seared as with a hot iron" so that things just do not bother you any more (1 Tim. 4:2). 1 can tell you one of the most valuable things you have, and that is not only a conscience, but a sensitive conscience. The way to develop a good conscience is always to tell the truth. So we hurt ourselves when we do not tell the truth. For one thing, as Mark Twain put it, you do not have to have such a good memory if you tell the truth, because a liar must have a good memory. "What was it I said? What did I say to that person? Ah, I think it was this." But if you always tell the truth, you do not need to worry about your memory.

I have had a lot to say in this book about sensitivity to the Holy Spirit and how easy it is to grieve the Spirit. This cannot be overemphasized. I long to be more sensitive than I am to the Holy Spirit. Two friends of mine in the Florida Keys—both of them bonefishing guides—entered into a prayer covenant to pray a specific thing for one another daily. I asked them to pray for me that I would become hypersensitive to the Holy Spirit. For this is what I want—almost more than anything. And when it comes to the ninth commandment, a consistent sensitivity to the Spirit will be what will enable us to carry out this command and not to violate it. What is more, we do not have to have such a good memory!

The problem is, then, when we begin to cover up we think, *What exactly was it I said? How did I say it?* And we get into all kinds of trouble. The downfall of President Nixon was not merely the Watergate event; it was the cover-up. And I think President Clinton also had a serious problem because people did not know what to believe about his integrity.

Have you ever had anybody lie about you? Have you had a word get back to you about what somebody said you said that was not true at all? I recently heard something that a prominent American had said about myself that was untrue (fortunately we have the whole thing on video). I had been in Toronto—that much was true—but he said that I was not able to preach at all and fell to the floor laughing. Not true. But he told this to a large audience in Kansas City. Somebody was there who told me about it and who happened to have been present at Toronto. But thousands of people will believe something like that. It hurts when people do not tell the truth.

Why do you suppose God gave us the ninth command? It reads, "You shall not give false testimony against your neighbor." The key phrase here is "give false testimony." It refers to giving accurate testimony in a court of law; that is the original meaning. It is not really a general command about truthfulness, that is to say, we are not under any obligation to reveal everything we know to anyone who asks. That is not what this command is saying. But we are to tell the truth when we do speak.

But when it comes to the New Testament, as always with every one of these commands, the New Testament goes quite beyond anything said in the Ten Commandments. So when it comes to this command about giving the truth, whereas the original occasion was about telling the truth under oath in a court of law, the New Testament tells us always simply to tell the truth. Paul said:

> Therefore each of you must put off falsehood and speak truthfully to his neighbor, for we are all members of one body.... Do not let any unwholesome talk come out of your mouths, but only what is helpful for building others up according to their needs, that it may benefit those who listen.
>
> —EPHESIANS 4:25, 29

So, if we walk in the Spirit, we will speak with honesty. Common sense would reveal this. Let me explain. The Bible says twice that it is impossible for God to lie; rather an extraordinary statement, if you ask me. It is in Titus 1:2: "God, who does not lie." And in Hebrews 6:18: "It is impossible for God to lie."

That is a wonderful thing about God. He is truth. You can believe everything He says, for the Bible is God's integrity on the line. You can believe the Bible; it is God's Word. It is impossible for God to lie.

The Holy Spirit is God. God the Father is God. God the Son is God. And because the Holy Spirit—the third person of the Trinity—is God, He cannot lie. Jesus called Him "the Spirit of truth" (John 14:16-17). Therefore if I walk in the Spirit, I will tell the truth. As we walk in the Spirit, we will be convicted along the way. Things that would not bother a person who does not have the Holy Spirit will bother the one who does have the Holy Spirit. The moment we are tempted to say something that might be an exaggeration or going a little further than the truth, the more we walk in the Spirit, the more we hear a warning sound inside. We will see, as it were, a flashing light, a warning, to be careful what we say. Because if I walk in the Spirit, I am going to tell the truth. This refers to our public testimony and what goes on in our private lives. As for myself, I desire always to preach and teach nothing but truth. I cannot think of anything worse for a person in my position than to propagate what is not absolutely true. This refers to doctrine and also how doctrine is applied—which is precisely what I am seeking to do in this book. If I preach in the Spirit, I am going to be upholding truth. And yet this begins in my personal, private life. If I walk in the Spirit, I will be transparently honest with people in relationships. This does not mean I blurt out all I know to be true but rather what I know is true that will be edifying. I will speak blessing into people's lives. Not flattery, but what is praiseworthy because it is true (Phil. 4:8).

REASONS FOR THE COMMANDMENT

Why, then, did God give this ninth commandment, "You shall not give false testimony against your neighbor"?

First, God wants His people to tell the truth when they speak. In ancient times two or three witnesses were required in a court of law. "One witness is not enough to convict a man accused of any crime or offense he may have committed. A matter must be established by the testimony of two or three witnesses" (Deut. 19:15). This was for the protection of anybody from being maligned by a personal enemy on a vendetta and who just wanted to bring another down. A person cannot be convicted unless two, and better, three, witnesses give testimony.

The second reason God gave this command is that He wants to protect us from being falsely accused. He does not like it if anybody lies about you. For it hurts. It hurts, and you say to yourself, "Why did they do it? It is not true." And then they tell it to someone else, and others believe the lie. You are cast down. But if you feel that way, so does God. This is your comfort when you are lied about. Are you prepared to believe this: that God cares even more than you do? God cares about His children.

If you are a parent, how do you feel if somebody says something about your child that is not true? I myself can handle many things said against me, but when I hear of something said against either of my children, I have to work hard to contain myself. The greatest testing I face is the way our own children are hurt.

If you do not like it when somebody says something against your child, especially something that is not true, you should know that God the Father feels that way about His children, too. Perhaps you have nobody who will defend you when people lie about you. But God heard it, and He does not like it. He said, "Vengeance is mine; I will repay." In other words, He will vindicate us. The word *vindicate* means "to have one's name cleared." I love this definition of vindication, for the doctrine of justification by faith comes to this. God clearing His own name comes to vindication. It's what God does best. Anything God does, He does well. But if He has an "area of expertise," it is this. This is because He calls Himself a God of justice, a God of truth. The most maligned person in the universe is God. He is the one who is lied about; He is the one who is hated; He is the one who is resented.

Maybe you resent God because He let you come into this world. Do you resent God because of His choice of parents for you? Do you resent God because of the particular class structure into which you were born? People say, "How could God have any integrity if He permits evil? How could God be God and not give everybody an equal chance?" God hears these charges. God feels it. But one day He will clear His name. And He will do it in such a way that the whole world will say, "Oh, I hadn't thought of that." But, you see, it is a blind spot that He has injected into the human race. The wisest philosopher cannot handle or deal satisfactorily with the question of evil. We are not going to understand it this side of heaven. But one day God will clear His name.

That blind spot is what makes faith a possibility. If we knew why God allowed evil, we would not need faith. But God has been pleased to decide that the just shall live by faith (Hab. 2:4). For that reason, we all have to wait for the final day when God will clear His name. No faith will be needed then.

A difference between a Christian and a non-Christian is this: the non-Christian says, "I want to see now how God will clear His name," but the Christian does it right now. I am prepared to state categorically that God is true, God is just, God is faithful; He keeps His word. Speaking personally, I have no complaints against Him. I have been in one situation after another where I thought there was no way that this too could work together for good, only to find after a short period of time I saw a reason for everything that happened.

> You do not have to train a baby how to lie!…And this is why God gave the command. All these commands are given because, by nature, we would do the very opposite of everything that is commanded.

If all of us can learn to lower our voices and say, "God is true," and vindicate Him now, we will not be blushing on the day of judgment when God clears His name.

There is a third reason God gave this command, and that is because it is hard to tell the truth, especially about ourselves. We get defensive. One illustration of how I can get defensive is in one of the weaknesses I have, in that sometimes my mind will wander. I do not know how many have a problem like that, but even sometimes my wife will say, "Did you hear me?"

And I will say, "Yes."

"Well, what did I say?"

And I will think, "You said—ah—"

"You were not listening, were you?"

It is not always easy to tell the truth.

I will say, in the end, "Well, no, I did not hear you." And it hurts.

You do not have to train a baby how to lie! The Bible says we came from our mother's womb speaking lies (Ps. 58:3). It is often easy to lie; it is often hard to tell the truth. And this is why God gave the command. All these commands are given because, by nature, we would do the very opposite of everything that is commanded.

Reason number four: God wants us to tell the truth about ourselves to Him. He wants each of us to develop an objectivity about ourselves and to be honest before Him. And yet the most foolish thing we can do is to wear the mask before God. "Nothing in all creation is hidden from God's sight. Everything is uncovered and laid bare before the eyes of him to whom we must give account" (Heb. 4:13).

When it comes to relationships we all wear the mask just a little bit. We do not want people to see us fully and openly and completely. The more we can take the mask off, the more we trust people, and the more we are not afraid for them to get to know us a little bit. We wear the mask as a defense mechanism so people might like us a little more. We are afraid they will not like us if they see us as we are.

But when it comes to our relationship with God, the sooner we learn to take the mask off, the better, because He sees beyond the mask. He sees right through us. It will not do to pretend.

A silly thing we can do is to try to convince God of what our motives are or to try to explain something to Him. There is something therapeutic I suppose about explaining something to God, about talking to Him, and that is all right up to a point. But if you think for one minute that we are informing Him of something, that we are giving Him some insight into ourselves, revealing something to Him, do not waste your time. He knows us all backward and forward, and He has a computer printout about our life and how we spend it. He remembers in detail everything that ever happened. He knows about our parents, about our childhood hurts—He knows all of those things. And so when we come before Him, there is no use pretending.

God wants us to tell the truth about ourselves, and that means you are going to admit that you are a sinner. The Bible says, "All have sinned and fall short of the glory of God" (Rom. 3:23). The way the King James Version refers to the parable of the sower in Luke 8 is that those who were of "an honest and good heart" received the word and bore fruit (Luke 8:15). An old friend of mine, Rolfe Barnard, preached a sermon once called, "Every Honest Person Will Go to Heaven." And people came out to hear that and thought, *What on earth is he going to say?* A lot of self-righteous people came saying, "I've been waiting for something like this for a long time, because I've always known that I was going to go to heaven. I've always known that I am an honest person." They came to listen to that sermon to get a little ammunition. But what Rolfe Barnard said was, "If you are really honest, you know that you are a sinner. If you are really honest, you know that Jeremiah got it right when he said, 'The heart is deceitful above all things, and desperately wicked: who can know it?' (Jer. 17:9, KJV). And if you are honest, you know your motives—why you do this, what is really behind it."

One day all motives will be revealed. "This will take place on the day when God will judge men's secrets through Jesus Christ, as my gospel declares" (Rom. 2:16). This is why God sent His Son into the world: we are basically a dishonest lot. Basically, we are deceitful. Basically, we are liars. Basically, we are self-righteous. We want to think that we do not need a substitute to take our place by dying on a cross. "I will negotiate with God directly without a mediator," some say. But that is dishonest and self-righteous. When we come to terms with ourselves, we will see how wonderful it is that God gave us a Savior who never sinned. Every day of His life Jesus lived without sinning. And for that reason, when He died on a cross and shed His blood, that blood satisfied God's justice. It came from One who spoke the truth and kept the ninth commandment in the richest possible manner.

A WARNING

This command also refers to a warning. "Do not give false testimony against your neighbor." The warning is this: the one who does will be punished. Moses went on to say, "Do not help a wicked man by being a malicious witness. Do not spread false reports."

> If a malicious witness takes the stand to accuse a man of a crime, the two men involved in the dispute must stand in the presence of the LORD before the priests and the judges who are in office at the time. The judges must make a thorough investigation, and if the witness proves to be a liar, giving false testimony against his brother, then do to him as he intended to do to his brother. You must purge the evil from among you. The rest of the people will hear of this and be afraid, and never again will such an evil thing be done among you. Show no pity: life for life, eye for eye, tooth for tooth, hand for hand, foot for foot.
> —DEUTERONOMY 19:16–21

The penalty for telling a lie in the Old Testament was rather like the Golden Rule in reverse. The Golden Rule is in Luke 6:31, where Jesus says, "Do to others as you would have them do to you." So when it comes to the penalty for telling a lie, God says that what you wanted to have happen to the other when you were lying will happen to you. So one is to be treated as he wished his neighbor would be treated.

Had the Mosaic Law been carried out, the accusers of Jesus would have been put to death. These were false accusations, and they couldn't get two or three witnesses. The funny but tragic irony is that the people who put Jesus to death were the great Law upholders. They were the ones who extolled the Law. You see the hypocrisy. They did not even go by the Law. It is often the case that those who are the most legalistic are the quickest to excuse sin.

THE JUDGMENT

The warning here is that the truth will come out. Listen to these words from Jesus: "There is nothing concealed that will not be disclosed, or hidden that will not be made known. What you have said in the dark will be heard in the daylight, and what you have whispered in the ear in the inner rooms will be proclaimed from the roofs" (Luke 12:2-3). "But I tell you that men will have to give account on the day of judgment for every careless word they have spoken" (Matt. 12:36). That verse scares me. I can't think of anything worse. Every careless word!

Abraham Lincoln said, "You may fool all the people some of the time; you can even fool some of the people all the time; but you can't fool all of the people all the time." The warning is that, at the judgment seat of Christ, everything will be revealed. There will come a time when there will be no more argument. You say now, "Did you say this?"

"No. What I said was this—"

"But I heard you say this."

"No, what I said was this—"

At the judgment, every mouth will be stopped and the truth will come out. It is going to be a terrible day when everything will be out in the open. This is why now is the time to begin to be honest and tell the truth—it will come out then. It will be far more painful then than now. At this moment there is mercy. If we know that we have been dishonest, swept the dirt under the carpet, lied about somebody, hurt somebody's reputation, been too defensive ourselves—"If we confess our sins, he is faithful and just and will forgive us our sins and purify us from all unrighteousness" (1 John 1:9).

God will give you a free pardon and a new beginning. He will say, "From this moment, walk in the Spirit."

The ninth command refers to the word *testimony*. "You shall not give false testimony against your neighbor." Jesus kept the ninth command in the richest possible way. We are talking about one man who was the embodiment of truth. "We beheld his glory, the glory as of the only begotten of the Father, full of grace and truth" (John 1:14, KJV). Jesus said, "I am the way and the truth and the life" (John 14:6). "He who speaks on his own does so to gain honor for himself, but he who works for the honor of the one who sent him is a man of truth; there is nothing false about him" (John 7:18).

We can therefore believe every word Jesus uttered. Jesus is God. It is impossible for God to lie. It was impossible for Jesus to lie. Because every word He said was mirroring what the Father told Him to say. That is why we can believe Him.

There is good news, and there is bad news. The bad news is that He will be your witness at the judgment. We are told in Acts 17:31 that God "will judge the world with justice by the man he has appointed." And He will tell the truth. None of us will get away with any kind of lie. He will step in and say, "Stop it! Here's what you said, here's what you did." And He will tell the truth. We are told in Revelation 1, "His eyes were like blazing fire" (Rev. 1:14). All that He feels about lying will come out then, because the devil is the father of lies (John 8:44). For once, the truth will come out.

The good news is that for those who have confessed Jesus He will also be a witness. He will plead your case before the Father and remind the Father of the prayer that He prayed in John 17:24, "Father, I will that they... be with me where I am" (KJV). And Jesus will remember the day you confessed Him. He will remember that moment when you said, "Yes." And He will know whether in your heart you were putting all of your trust in His blood and in His righteousness, that you were trusting Him for salvation.

So on that awful, horrible day—it is impossible to exaggerate the horror of that day of judgment—everything will be revealed. Jesus will speak the truth, and He will be your witness. Those who have Him on their side will be spared the eternal condemnation that awaits those who have not confessed Jesus.

GUIDED BY THE SPIRIT

In the meantime we have the witness of the Holy Spirit. For He is called "the Spirit of truth" (John 14:17). In John 16:13 Jesus said, "He will guide you into all truth." The moment you come to Christ and invite Him in and confess your sins you will receive the Holy Spirit. Sometimes when the Spirit comes it is a conscious experience and people can remember it as long as they live. Other times, the Holy Spirit comes in and a person feels nothing, but his outlook is different and he is conscious that he has put his trust in Jesus. He just knows something has happened; he has passed from death to life (John 5:24).

The Holy Spirit will be with you. He will not desert you. And He will guide you into all truth. You do not need to worry; the Holy Spirit will not deceive you. As long as you have a heart to do God's will, you will be kept from serious mistakes and error. The Bible says, "If anyone chooses to do God's will, he will find out whether my teaching comes from God or whether I speak on my own" (John 7:17). You will be spared the embarrassment of serious theological mistakes or error. That is the wonderful thing about having the Holy Spirit; He will guide you into all truth.

My hobby is bonefishing, which is a sport because bonefish are caught for fun. They are very hard to catch. It combines hunting and fishing simultaneously. You do not usually eat bonefish; they are too bony—hence the name.

I became fascinated the moment I heard of bonefishing. I had heard stories about it and read about it in some fishing magazines. So I went to a fishing camp in Key Largo, Florida. "I want to do some bonefishing," I said to the manager. "Will you rent me a boat?" "Are you a bonefisherman?" he asked. "Will be after today," I naïvely replied. "Nobody goes bonefishing for the first time without a guide," he said.

I did not want to pay the price for a guide; besides, I did not want to admit I needed a guide. But the manager was right. I tried on my own—couldn't even find them or see them (if they were there). I gave in, hired a guide, and, lo and behold, he took me to the exact same place where I had been trying for months. In minutes he began to see them and eventually enabled me to know what they really looked like and how to spot them. It was a thrilling experience to see a bonefish for myself—and to hook one. But it was impossible without a guide. Jesus promised that the Holy Spirit would be our guide. "He will guide you into all truth" (John 16:13). Why is it necessary to have the Spirit as a guide? He shows what is there—in the Word that, without the Spirit, we cannot see. "The man without the Spirit does not accept the things that come from the Spirit of God, for they are foolishness to him, and he cannot understand them, because they are spiritually discerned" (1 Cor. 2:14). But we too must pay a price—self-denial and the willingness to admit we cannot grasp holy things by ourselves without the Spirit.

This ninth command, "You shall not give false testimony against your neighbor," is fulfilled in the New Testament by our walk. John talks about "walking in the light" (1 John 1:7). John says, "It has given me great joy to find some of your children walking in the truth" (2 John 4). Galatians 5:25 talks about "keep[ing] in step with the Spirit." The Holy Spirit, who is God, will convict you along the way. For example, you will be given a dislike of things such as exaggeration. You will develop a sensitivity. You will think of your own achievements not in terms of embellishing them and making people think more highly of you. The way you regard yourself will be affected. You will develop an objectivity, and you will be convicted. This is why it is so important to develop a sensitive conscience.

The worst thing that can happen to a person is to be given over to strong delusion, as in 2 Thessalonians 2:11, where they believe a lie. The Christian lives a life in the Spirit that will make him honest. A life without the Spirit means deceit. Proverbs 14:25: "A truthful witness saves lives, but a false witness is deceitful."

Your witness will be in a courtroom, and that courtroom is the whole world.

Chapter 15

THE TENTH COMMANDMENT:
THE SIN THAT CONDEMNS US ALL

You shall not covet your neighbor's house. You shall not covet your neighbor's wife, or his manservant or maidservant, his ox or donkey, or anything that belongs to your neighbor.

—EXODUS 20:17

I REMEMBER ONCE FISHING with my friend Harlan Milby. Harlan is a successful businessman—cautious but also a risk taker. Everything he touches seems to turn to gold. One of the things he likes to do is to set people up in business and give them a good start. He began telling me about different people I knew—old friends from college days—whom he had helped. One of them became a multimillionaire in the end. I used to think that I was untouched by greed and the desire for material things. I never wanted a yacht, an expensive car, or a luxurious house. But that is almost certainly because I knew I never would get those things anyway, so such a temptation was remote. As Harlan was telling about one person after another who had nothing at one time but who now—because of his help—became financially independent, I began to seethe within. I finally got enough courage to ask, "Why have you never done anything like that for me?" He replied without any blushing whatsoever, "I never felt led to." He went on to say that he knew I was called to be a preacher and that he did not want me to get off track by going outside my calling. This did not make me happy, but it should have.

And yet it made me see how hypocritical I had been—even playing games with myself—by thinking I was unattracted to material things. I saw how attracted I was to such after all. For what I was doing as he spoke is called coveting. It made me see what a sinner I am after all. And that shows the main purpose of the tenth commandment: to reveal the heart. When we see what we are really like, it is not a pretty sight.

This command condemns us all. You may have thought that up to now you could keep these commands—and there is a sense in which that could be quite true. But...this command covers everything imaginable.

Each of the Ten Commandments has this in common: they all point to a righteousness that we would never naturally want to attain. First of all, mankind would never know what God's standard of righteousness was, and we would never even think about it. The Law was given that we might see something of God's will for His people. It is needed because we are a fallen race; we were born into sin and shaped in iniquity because of the sin of Adam, our first parent. None of us come into this world as Adam was created before the Fall. The condition in which he left the Garden of Eden after the Fall is what all of us have inherited.

The word *covet* means to desire eagerly, especially something that is not your own and especially something that belongs to another person. This command condemns us all. You may have thought that up to now you could keep these commands—and there is a sense in which that could be quite true. But what God did, in speaking to Moses, was to give a final word that makes us all see that we are sinners—we are all condemned. This command covers everything imaginable.

God starts out by saying, "You must not covet your neighbor's house." So He begins by referring to another person's dwelling place. He says, "You cannot even inwardly desire that person's dwelling place"—wishing his or her house were yours. God says, "No. Don't even think about it."

Then He moves from there: "You shall not covet your

neighbor's wife." This refers to lust. The reason Jesus could interpret the seventh command as He did was because of this tenth command. Jesus said, "You have heard that it was said, 'Do not commit adultery.' But I tell you that anyone who looks at a woman lustfully has already committed adultery with her in his heart" (Matt. 5:28). So if you wish that you had another man's wife—do not even think about it, says the tenth commandment. You are not allowed to think along those lines because that is sin. You must not think, *I do not think that man appreciates his wife.* Or, *I do not think that woman is treated as she should be.* Or, *I do not think that woman appreciates her husband. If only I were married to him, I could be the perfect wife for him.* Don't even think about it. Don't let yourself begin to imagine, *If only I had that person, I could make them so much happier.* It is not OK, says the tenth commandment.

God goes on from there to say, "You shall not covet your neighbor's manservant or maidservant." Even if you do not have a servant, you will not wish that you had someone else's. Don't even think about that, or even think of bribing that person by saying, "I will let you work for me—I will give you more money." It is possible that a person can scout around "head-hunting" and saying, "I will give you more money." Well, according to this you are coveting what is not yours.

Don't covet a person's ox or donkey. You may or may not have an ox or a donkey. You may never have wanted an ox or a donkey. But had you been living then, this matter would come home to you. Or perhaps you have wanted to own the equivalent of that, considering how that may relate today. An ox or donkey was used as a means of transportation as well as livelihood. It was also like collateral—or money in the bank. Have you ever been envious of another's car, hobby, or ability to make money? That is what this tenth commandment is about. But suppose you were living then? And you owned a few animals. But if you saw a better quality in your neighbor's animals, forget about it and do not think about it. They do not belong to you.

We could go down the list, and He could have come up with many other things, but what God does is to summarize it by saying, "You shall not covet anything that belongs to your neighbor." So whatever that person possesses, do not even think about it—it is a sin to want it.

You may say, "This is not fair." But this is God's Word. He has given us His Word, and there is a reason for it.

In some ways, this command is unique. It is certainly the sharpest and most powerful of the Ten Commandments.

THE REASONS FOR THIS COMMANDMENT

What is the reason for the tenth command? The first is, to nip sin in the bud. Let me explain what I mean by that. The eighth commandment says, "You shall not steal." But the tenth command says, "Don't even think about stealing." You are not allowed to want what is someone else's.

We learn a lot from this because, when it comes to temptation, the way to deal with temptation is, first, not even to think about it. Temptation begins in the mind, and the very fact that God says, "You shall not covet," is implicitly helping us to see how to deal with temptation. Temptation is what leads to sin. Sin is the result of giving in to temptation. And if you will take seriously the tenth command, you will recognize you are not even allowed to think about those things that you know go right against what God wants.

The second reason for this command is that it internalizes the previous nine commandments. What I mean by that is this. Apart from this tenth commandment, you could keep the first nine. Even an unregenerate person, an unsaved person, an unconverted person, can keep the first nine commands to an extent. It is the tenth command that condemns us all. The first nine commands say, "You must not sin." But the tenth command says, "You must not want to sin."

You may say, "Look, I can't help it. I want to. It is not fair. It goes right against my natural desires. God is being unfair to me."

If we have learned anything about these commands in this book, we have learned this: every single one of them is for our good. God knows exactly what He is doing. And if we can learn from this word, our lives will be changed. It is the most powerful of the Ten Commandments.

The third reason for this command is: it refers to the heart. It is the only one of the commandments to refer to the heart.

The word *heart* is not explicitly referred to in the Book of Exodus. But when we get to the Book of Deuteronomy, and Moses begins to elaborate on the commands, he brings in this word *heart*. Now that was implied without using the word, because the word *covet* refers to something that we desire from inside. That is what gave Jesus the rationale for the way He interpreted the Law. Jesus said that murder happens in your heart even if you do not kill a person. Adultery happens in the heart even if you do not physically sleep with another woman. And because He said that, we understand what we are all capable of doing. He could say that because He was simply taking the tenth commandment and applying it to the others.

We could go down the list of the other nine commands, using the tenth as the introduction, and then we would begin to see how we are guilty of breaking all of these commands. If it were not for the tenth commandment, we could probably, at least to a great extent, keep every single one of the commandments.

It is interesting to talk to people who think they understand the Ten Commandments, and you find that they probably know two or three of them. The first one people think of is, "You shall not commit adultery." They may think of "You shall not steal," "You shall not murder," and that is as far as they go. Most can't remember many more. And they think that because they have not killed anybody or slept with another woman, and they do not steal and try to be honest—they assume that they keep the Ten Commandments.

The fourth reason this command is given, then, is to show that we are sinners. This is the command that convicted the great apostle Paul (Rom. 7:7–11). Paul once said that before he was converted, as for the righteousness of the Law, he was blameless (Phil. 3:4–6). He was actually referring to the first nine commandments. When it comes to those nine, perhaps you too believe that you are without sin.

I have talked to many people on the streets. From having witnessed on the streets around Westminster Chapel since 1982, we got to know what people are like, and we knew almost all the questions they would ask. I have talked to all kinds of people, and they look me straight in the face and say to me that they are not sinners. Many even say, "I've never done anything wrong." Arthur Blessitt always replies, "Come on, now, you are smarter than that!" For people know at bottom that they are far from perfect.

The reason they can do this, then, is because they will usually take two or three commands and think that if they are not giving in to those sins they are OK. The easiest thing in the world is for a person to come up with something that he thinks is wrong, and if he does not do that, he feels quite OK.

A friend of mine, Jack Brothers, who is now in heaven with the Lord, was a bonefish guide in the Florida Keys. Jack was an alcoholic, and it took him a long time to admit that he really was an alcoholic. The hardest thing for a person who has a drinking problem is to admit that he or she really is an alcoholic. That word makes a person think, *Well, I am not that! I drink a little bit, but I am not that!* Jack was one of those who would not admit that he was an alcoholic. The only thing that brought him to admit it (after people had warned him over and over again) was when he got into so much trouble that he had no choice but to go to an Alcoholics Anonymous meeting. And as a result of that, he finally uttered the words, "My name is Jack Brothers, and I am an alcoholic." That was a major step for him. The funny thing is that it also was a great impediment in trying to get him to come to Christ. The reason for that was because he had not had a drink in eleven years, even though every day he would admit that he was an alcoholic and would pray, "God, get me through this day without a drink." Then at the end of every day before he went to bed, he would sit on the edge of his bed and say, "God, thank You that I got through this day without a drink." He had really gone eleven years without a drink. But when I tried to lead Jack to Christ, the problem was that he couldn't see that he was a sinner. To him, not drinking was such a big, big thing—that he couldn't see anything else wrong with him.

There are a lot of people like that. They have overcome some bad habit, and they think it is such an accomplishment that the thought of being sinful is out of the question.

The reason for this command, therefore, is to make a person

come to terms with what they truly know in their hearts. The apostle Paul—this man who always thought he was blameless (Phil. 3:6)—said in Romans 7:7, "I would not have known what coveting really was if the law had not said, 'Do not covet.'" In other words, he is saying, "I would not have known what sin was; I would not have known what lust was. As a result of that tenth command," he says, "that got me! That hit me right between the eyes."

THE TRUTH ABOUT OURSELVES

Obviously, the Holy Spirit was at work in Paul. For even the tenth commandment must be applied by the Spirit. Because if you are not saved, what God wants you to see is that you have sinned before Him. I can reason with you and show you from the tenth commandment that you are a sinner, because if you hate, according to Jesus, you have committed murder. If you lust, you have committed adultery. But that may not bother you because you say, "I do not see any problem there. I do not see anything wrong with that." But when the Holy Spirit takes the same words and applies them, you see as Paul saw that you really are a sinner. Paul said, "Sin, seizing the opportunity afforded by the commandment, produced in me every kind of covetous desire" (Rom. 7:8). And, he says, "I realized what I was like." He said, "When this came, sin sprang to life." He realized what he was like; he said, "I died."

Self-righteous people manage to go right through the first nine of these commandments and feel no conviction at all, but if you are totally honest, you will have to admit that this is the sin that condemns us all. James put it like this in his epistle, "For whoever keeps the whole law and yet stumbles at just one point is guilty of breaking all of it" (James 2:10).

You may wish there hadn't been a tenth commandment. Why did God give ten? Why didn't He just give the first nine? You may think God said, "Well, I've given nine, so let us just round it off to ten and come up with another one—what shall it be?" Maybe you wish He had said, "Spend more time in prayer," as the tenth commandment. Maybe you wish He had said, "Go to church or the synagogue more than you do." Maybe you wish He had said, "Tithe your income." Maybe you wish He had said, "Be good to old people." Maybe you wish He had said, "Pray for leaders." I could go down a list on various good things, but what God did in His infinite wisdom is to give a command that, if we see it as it is, will make us see that we have not kept all of the nine that just preceded it. God says we are sinners.

Some years ago Dr. Lloyd-Jones told me that he went to a dentist and found out that this dentist was a leading Jehovah's Witness. The dentist learned that Dr. Lloyd-Jones was a minister, and the doctor gave the dentist one of his books. It was his book on Romans chapter 3. The dentist, out of courtesy, began to read Dr. Lloyd-Jones's book. There was a place in the book—and I have read it—where Dr. Lloyd-Jones was commenting on the verse, "That every mouth might be stopped God concluded all under sin." The doctor wrote, "Has your mouth ever been stopped?" The dentist read that, and the next time Dr. Lloyd-Jones came for treatment, the dentist looked at him and said, "I have been reading your book."

"Well," said Dr. Lloyd-Jones, "what do you think?"

He said, "I think you can say I've been born again!"

The dentist said that those words, "Have you ever had your mouth stopped?," made him realize that he had gone on talking and no one had stopped his mouth. He said, "My mouth has been stopped." He had come to terms with the hollowness of his life, the emptiness of his arguments, and the superficiality of his thinking. He bowed to the truth.

I ask you that. Has your mouth ever been stopped? What God wants to do is to make you stop and think: where will you spend eternity? Think: where will you be five minutes after you die? The Bible makes us see that we are sinners.

There is a further relevance of this command. What other sins does this touch upon?

There is self-pity. Are you aware that self-pity is a sin? This command puts the finger on our self-pity. When we think of things we do not have that other people do have, we begin to feel sorry for ourselves. When my friend Harlan was telling me about those old classmates of mine who were now successful in making money, I was not only coveting but also feeling sorry for myself. I felt it also later that day when I got out of his Porsche and stepped into my old Pontiac that had almost no brakes. Has this happened to you too? God says, "Stop it!" to all of us. Self-pity is not allowed by this commandment.

Jealousy. This is the command that makes us see that jealousy is a sin. Another person has something that we do not have, and we begin to be envious and think, *Why do they have it and I do not?* That is jealousy; it is sin. This is the command that internalizes all of the other commands.

Lust. As Paul said, "I wouldn't have known what lust was if it hadn't been for this particular command." This is why Jesus could say, "If you lust, you have already committed adultery." For in the heart the sin is there. You may not be sent to jail for it or lose your job. But before God you desire a woman—or a man—who is not yours. The truth is we have all done that. It is the tenth commandment that unveils the heart. For coveting a sexual relationship that violates God's Law is lust. This command that brought Paul to his knees is what exposes us all.

This is the command that makes you see greed. You are not happy with what you have. And you are determined to have more and more.

It is the sin that puts the finger on pride. Why is it that you want to keep up with the Joneses? Why is it you go into debt for things that you do not really want? Just to make people envious of you? Are you spending money that you do not have for things you do not need to make people you do not like admire you? It is pride.

And this points to the sin of laziness. We do not want to work for something; we just covet it. We get angry with the person for having it; we get angry with God. We are angry inside, and we would rather not have to work. This command implicitly shows how we must work by the sweat of our brow. It is by hard work that we are to get things we need, and that way we feel good because God gave us those things.

Complaining. God hates murmuring. In 1 Corinthians 10 God put sexual immorality and murmuring on the same plane. Most people today wouldn't do that; most people would think that sexual immorality is the worst sin. In some ways it is because of the social implications and the way it scandalizes. But complaining, in the eyes of God, is just as bad. Are you a complainer? Do you murmur? "Why is it I do not have these things that others do?" Murmuring, at bottom, is directed to God. "Why has God led me this way?" "Why did He let this happen?" "Why does He bless others but not me?"

Idolatry. The Bible calls covetousness "idolatry" (Col. 3:5). Why? We want what we can't have rather than desiring what we can have—God Himself.

The relevance for all of us in this is not only to make us see how sinful we are, but also to teach us to be content. We can learn from this command. The apostle Paul said:

> But godliness with contentment is great gain. For we brought nothing into the world, and we can take nothing out of it. But if we have food and clothing, we will be content with that. People who want to get rich fall into temptation and a trap and into many foolish and harmful desires that plunge men into ruin and destruction. For the love of money is a root of all kinds of evil. Some people, eager for money, have wandered from the faith and pierced themselves with many griefs.
>
> —1 TIMOTHY 6:6–10

There are those who have made professions of faith in Christ but then have let the desire for money and material things creep in. They once had warm hearts toward God and developed a sensitivity for godly things, but before they know it, things get in, and they begin to want this and that. They begin to say, "God made me this way; this is natural. He understands my natural feelings." They justify themselves every inch of the way.

"The backslider in heart shall be filled with his own ways: and a good man shall be satisfied from himself" (Prov. 14:14, KJV). That means that once you can see no wrong, anything now becomes all right. We begin to justify everything we do and make ourselves the exception to the rule. The favorite trick of the devil is to say, "You are the exception. Other people couldn't do this, but in your case it is OK."

This command should teach us to be content and remember

that God will give us what we need—by hard work and by accepting from His hand what He pleases. It is a wonderful thing to come to terms with this. God knows what I need, and I will get it.

Sometimes I look at this and say to myself, "Why can't I have that? Why is it that other people get to be blessed financially and I cannot be blessed?" It is so easy, if we are not careful, to fall into the sin of self-pity. But then God graciously shakes me by the shoulders and says, "RT, you have everything you need."

That is the promise to every one of my readers. God will give you everything you need. "No good thing does he withhold from those whose walk is blameless" (Ps. 84:11). This command should help us to see that and help us learn contentment. Whatever you see that another person owns or another person has, whether his wife, her husband, or those things—leave them alone, and do not even think about them.

I have to say that if we come under this tenth command we will get an intense experience of what sin is like. When we come to terms with the implications of this sharp, powerful, profound, command—"Do not covet"—we begin to realize that this is what we are doing, and we think, *Oh, I did not realize that I am like I am.* It is like peeling the layers of an onion, when we find more and more about ourselves, and think, *I can't believe that this is me!*

THE PERFECTION OF JESUS

Is there a remedy for this sin? This sin makes us see that we are all sinners. We all know what it is to want what is not ours. We all know what it is to lust in our hearts. We all know what it is to hate and not forgive. We all know what it is to complain. We all know what it is to murmur. God sent His Son into the world— who never lusted, who never complained, who was not lazy, who did everything exactly right. He did not give in to pride. There was nothing flowing in His veins but the purest love. We are told that He was tempted at all points just as we are. When we get to heaven, we will find that His temptation was stronger than any of ours. Why? Because He was a perfect man. All of us have been shaped by imperfect parents; we are not whole. Nobody is perfect sexually. No one is perfect in his perception and outlook. None of us are perfect in the way we see people. Jesus was the perfect man, and His temptation was all the more intense.

Jesus never sinned. For that reason, when He died on the cross He was in a position to pay our debts, because He presented to the Father the righteousness that you and I could not produce. God was looking for a righteous people—and He couldn't find any. He looked high and low over the earth. John, writing the Book of Revelation on the island of Patmos, looked in heaven to see if anybody was worthy to open the scroll and its seven seals. He saw Abraham, Isaac, and Jacob. He saw Ezekiel and Daniel, and He said, "I wept because no one was found who was worthy." (See Revelation 5:2–5.)

You can read the lives of the great saints and find that they are all ordinary people. I've had the privilege of knowing some of the greatest Christian men of the twentieth century—I am just lucky that I got to know them and that I rubbed shoulders with them. And I have discovered that they are all just men—the best of men are men at best. Abraham lied about his wife. Moses was a murderer. King David was an adulterer. I could go on and on.

God said, "None of these people will do." But He sent His Son, Jesus Christ, who made it without sin right to the end. His most severe temptation was in the last three hours of His life. The devil used anybody there to get some retaliation out of Him. They said, "He saved others; He cannot save Himself. Son of God, come down from the cross so we can see and believe!" They were needling Him by saying anything so that He would just say one retaliatory word. Had He said one word back, the whole plan would have shut down.

But right to the end, Jesus resisted. And then as He breathed His last, He said, "It is finished!" (John 19:31). In that moment the righteousness that He had was imputed to the whole world (2 Cor. 5:19). All we have to do to receive that righteousness is to trust what He did on that cross. He was our substitute; He never coveted. Jesus lived only for the glory of His Father.

"Coveting" the Things of God

However, God allows for a new kind of coveting. This command, "You must not covet," nonetheless points to a legitimate kind of coveting. For example, thirsting for God. David said, "My soul thirsts for God, for the living God" (Ps. 42:2). This is what God will do for you—He will give you a thirst for Himself. This command shows that we can have a desire for things that God wants us to have more of, such as a longing for good fellowship. You could be keeping company with people who are not good for you. Your best friends will be in the family of God. They may not be perfect, but it is true that the things that will mean most to you in life will come from your associations with those who love the Lord.

God will give you a desire to please Him. Paul even said, "But eagerly desire the greater gifts" (1 Cor. 12:31). You can have a thirst for more of the Spirit and the gifts, the fruit, and the power of the Spirit. God says, "That is OK."

Paul said, "So I say, live by the Spirit, and you will not gratify the desires of the sinful nature" (Gal. 5:16). Do you want to know how you can fulfill the command "you shall not covet"? By walking in the Spirit. Let me explain. The Holy Spirit is God. God is content. God is not jealous of anybody. God is not envious of anybody. God does not want anything anybody else has; He is happy in Himself. When you walk in the Spirit, you too are happy. It is amazing—when you walk in the Spirit, the things you wanted so much simply leave you! God will do this for all of us.

One last thing. Recalling my envy and self-pity over my old friends being helped by Harlan, I have now lived long enough to witness two things. First, God has over the years given me an appetite for a greater anointing. I now want it so much that I thank God my friend Harlan wouldn't set me up in business. My calling has stayed on track and with it a desire for more of the Holy Spirit. Second, I have also lived long enough to see what has happened to some of those people who were so well off financially. As Paul said, such people, "eager for money, have wandered from the faith and pierced themselves with many griefs" (1 Tim. 6:10). I wouldn't trade places with any of them now.

Notes

INTRODUCTION

1. R. T. Kendall, *Calvin and English Calvinism to 1647* (Oxford: Oxford University Press, 1979).
2. Ibid.
3. Ibid.

CHAPTER 1
A STUNNING CLAIM

1. "From the days of John the Baptist until now, the kingdom of heaven has been forcefully advancing, and forceful men lay hold of it" (Matt. 11:12, NIV). I fear this translation interprets more than translates the Greek. This translation coheres with the idea that taking the kingdom "by storm" is a good thing, even right to do.
2. R. T. Kendall, *He Saves* (London: Hodder & Stoughton, 1989).
3. Cecil F. Alexander, "There Is a Green Hill Far Away." Public domain.

CHAPTER 2
THE DESTINY OF THE LAW

1. An ancient Christological controversy centered on this letter *iota*. The two Greek words *homoousion* and *homoiousion* look much the same, but the latter includes the iota, which translates "like" as opposed to the former "the same." The followers of Arius said Jesus was like God; the followers of Athanasius said He was the same God. The iota of difference was vast indeed. Thankfully, the Athanasians won, and this became standard orthodoxy for the church ever since.

CHAPTER 5
THE REASON FOR THE TEN COMMANDMENTS

1. Ludwig Feuerbach, *Das Wesen des Christentums* (1841), translated into English (*The Essence of Religion*, by George Eliot, 1853, 2nd ed. 1881).

2. Lidie H. Edmunds, "My Faith Has Found a Resting Place." Public domain.

CHAPTER 6
THE FIRST COMMANDMENT:
THE TRUE GOD

1. "Feuerbach, Ludwig Andreas," Microsoft Encarta Online Encyclopedia, 2005 http://encarta.msn.com © 1997–2005 Microsoft Corporation.

CHAPTER 7
THE SECOND COMMANDMENT:
THE HIDDENNESS OF GOD

1. Elizabeth C. Clephane, "Beneath the Cross of Jesus." Public domain.

CHAPTER 8
THE THIRD COMMANDMENT:
THE NAME OF GOD

1. William Shakespeare, *Othello*, Act 3, Scene 3.
2. Graham Kendrick and Chris Robinson, "Restore, O Lord," copyright © 1981 Thankyou Music (admin. by EMI Christian Music Publishing). Used by permission.
3. H. W. Fowler, Della Thompson, and F. G. Fowler, eds., *The Concise Oxford Dictionary of Current English* (Oxford: Oxford University Press, 9th edition, 1995).

CHAPTER 9
THE FOURTH COMMANDMENT:
IS SUNDAY SPECIAL?

1. Institutes II: viii: 33, 34.
2. Ibid. XXIII, viii.

Strengthen
YOUR FAITH WALK!

We pray that you have a fresh, new understanding of grace and that you have been blessed by this teaching. Dr. Kendall has several other messages which will refresh you along your journey.

A beautiful devotional beyond description...

The absolute perfect gift for someone you love or for yourself, this compilation of conversations with God covers thousands of years of heartfelt prayers by people like St. Augustine, Martin Luther, Andrew Murray, Oswald Chambers, and more.

1-59185-804-6 / $14.99

Experience thanksgiving every day!

This book tackles a long-neglected subject but one that is central to our faith—being thankful to God and to each other. Learn how to make these two words have meaning in your life—"with thanksgiving."

1-59185-627-2 / $13.99

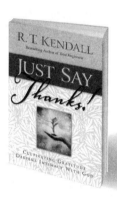

Forgive and forget!

When everything in you wants to hold a grudge, point a finger, and remember the pain, God wants you to lay it all aside. "This is a book that should be read around the world." —D. James Kennedy, PhD. Senior Minister, Coral Ridge Presbyterian Church

0-88419-889-8 / $13.99

Call 800-599-5750 now and Mention Offer #BP6201.
Or visit www.charismahouse.com to save 25%!

5654

Strang Communications,
publisher of both **Charisma House** and
Charisma magazine, wants to give you

3 FREE ISSUES
of our **award-winning** magazine.

WWW.CHARISMAMAG.COM

Since its inception in 1975 *Charisma* magazine has helped thousands of Christians stay connected with what God is doing worldwide.

Within its pages you will discover in-depth reports and the latest news from a Christian perspective, biblical health tips, global events in the body of Christ, personality profiles, and so much more. Join the family of *Charisma* readers who enjoy feeding their spirits each month with miracle-filled testimonies and inspiring articles that bring clarity, provoke prayer, and demand answers.

To claim your **3 free issues** of *Charisma*, send your name and address to: Charisma 3 Free Issues Offer, 600 Rinehart Road, Lake Mary, FL 32746. Or you may call **1-800-829-3346** and ask for Offer # **96FREE**. This offer is only valid in the USA.

Charisma
+CHRISTIAN LIFE
www.charismamag.com

5567